MEXICAN AND CENTRAL AMERICAN MYTHOLOGY

MEXICAN AND CENTRAL AMERICAN MYTHOLOGY

Irene Nicholson

PAUL HAMLYN · LONDON

CONTENTS

COLOUR PLATES

Uniform with this edition:
Greek Mythology
Egyptian Mythology
North American Indian Mythology
Indian Mythology

Paul Hamlyn Limited
Drury House Russell Street
London WC2

INTRODUCTION

Quetzalcoatl, the plumed serpent, was represented in every artistic medium. This image appears repeatedly on his pyramid at Teotihuacán, where the great size produces an aggressive effect that belies the gentle and compassionate nature of this god. Eighth century A.D.

The myths of Mexico and Central America create a world compact of jewels and flowers and birds, bright as a kaleidoscope and as everchanging. No single event can be trapped by logic because the myths belong to another world, both more instinctive and more emotional. Each god can be his twin or his corollary. Each story can be interpreted in several different ways according to the context and the reader's understanding. The symbols are few and concentrated, manipulated with such economy that each is made to serve a wide range of philosophical and religious ideas; and this device helps to stress the underlying unity of all knowledge, the relativity of subjective truth against the permanence of the objective, itself far from immobile but alive and vibrating about its still centre.

The images used as symbols are limited and may even seem monotonous until we begin to search for their deeper meanings. Shells, jewels, flowers, birds, maize, hearts, arrows, thorns of cacti: these keep recurring; but they are skilfully handled to produce all the concepts needed for a lofty philosophy and a complete cosmology, both of which are entirely at variance with the mistaken idea that the basic religion of middle America was founded on human sacrifice and the tearing out of hearts.

The human acts of blood rituals and licensed homicide came later, and were a distortion of what must once have been an extraordinarily complete vision of the place of man and of organic life in the universe.

If the gods had possessed names as easy to pronounce as Venus and Hermes, and if the stories had been handed down to us in more coherent form instead of piecemeal, usually gathered by friars who – in spite of their laudable efforts to preserve the ancient ideas – could scarcely have been expected to understand them or be sympathetic toward them, they might by now be as familiar to every school child as those of the Greeks and Romans. But we stumble over Cinteotl (Cin-te-otl); Huitzilopochtli (Huitz-i-lopoch-tli) is a tongue-twister; and it is bothersome to have to unravel the exact relationship between Quetzalcoatl (Quetzal-co-atl) and Ehecatl (E-he-catl) – both of them gods of wind among other things, and up to a certain point interchangeable. The picture becomes even more difficult when gods and men acquire a single identity, as when Quetzalcoatl the plumed serpent becomes identified with Topiltzin, a real-life figure born in the latter part of the tenth century who was the last king of the Toltecs.

None of the problems presented by the myths of Mexico and Central America is really insuperable provided we refuse to be caught up in needless detail and can see the broad principles upon which the stories were built. Created would be a misleading word to use, because these myths seem to rise out of that deep well of knowledge lying unfathomed in the human mind – hidden by that logical brain so overworked in many of the activities of modern life. Fundamentally the stories have a simplicity of intention that gives them the directness of a deliberately wrought and profound work of art. We shall, therefore, try to keep the picture as clear as possible and shall make no attempt to sort out, list and enumerate all the hundreds of names of gods that can be reduced in the last analysis to one – and on a less unified level to a few of the basic aspects of this all-powerful creator of the universe – Ometeotl.

It is important to let the religious, philosophical, and cosmological concepts speak for themselves. When they have done so, we shall see just how it happened – inevitably and tragically – that a religion of love and of consciousness became debased into a cult of the master race.

We need here to beware of a rather odd argument that has sometimes been advanced to explain the human sacrifices in the midst of a religion whose inner aim was the same as that of all great systems of thought: consciousness, love, and union with the creator of the universe. The argument goes something like this: Aztec sacrifices were not a religious perversion, but represented the heights of worship in the western hemisphere. Europeans ought to be able to understand this, because the western world does not consider the crucifixion of Christ as perversion. We have no right from our vantage point in the twentieth century to assume that human sacrifice is necessarily degenerate and immoral.

But this argument refuses to admit the existence – beneath our subjectively formed social rules of behaviour – of an objective voice within us which, if we listened to it attentively, would tell us the difference between real and changing right and wrong. To admit that other, subjective and very unreliable voices can easily be mistaken for it is not to say that a basic distinction between right and wrong does not exist. It is a little difficult to see how the practice of slaughtering enemies wholesale and with particularly cruel and painful techniques, in order to satisfy deities in heaven, could ever be condoned by a responsible elite or priesthood anywhere in the world.

A Zapotec funerary urn. The head represents a jaguar, the form given to the god Tepeyollotl who was 'Heart of the Mountain' and propitiated as being the cause of earthquakes. The Zapotecs were unlike most of the Mexican peoples, being more peaceful and speaking a different tongue, but like the others their religion was dominated by the figure of the plumed serpent. Fourteenth-century clay.

The Zapotec culture was eclipsed by the Mixtec, one product of which was the intricately decorated walls of the great palace at Mitla. The motifs have a meaning which also appears in the *Codex Zouche-Nuttall*, but their application in architectural terms has not so far been determined. Eighth to eleventh centuries A.D.

A toy, or possibly a votive offering, from Nopiloa. The wheel was not used by the Aztecs at the time of the Conquest; kings and nobles were carried in litters and war was fought on foot, probably because of the difficult nature of the ground in much of the realm. But this figure shows that the wheel was known. Totonac, sixth to ninth centuries A.D.

A ceremonial axehead in marble, with a deer seated within the headdress. Fom the Veracruz region.

Intentionally or otherwise, this argument has also the effect of reversing the whole idea of the crucifixion and of the Aztec sacrifices. It reverses, as it were, the arrow of events. Aztec sacrifices were a central ritual of the religion itself, though not in its original form. It became debased, and those who were sacrificed were not the misunderstood, maligned, and martyred; but the hapless enemy tribes who, according to the view of the master race, could quite well be sacrificed to feed the sun god. It would be difficult to find in history another religion that made the massacre of enemies not merely a common practice but a central ritual. Christian ritual is *not* based on the killing of an enemy but on the perpetuation of Christ's martyrdom, killed as he was by the *enemies* of his religion. The Aztec sacrifices simply cannot, in other words, be explained away by a kind of sleight-of-hand that turns the enemies of a religion into its most faithful adherents.

Another very general illusion is that the Aztec and Maya myths are those of a primitive people who wanted better crops, rain in due season, and sunshine to whiten the silken beards of maize. This kind of naive philosophy was very likely the outermost clothing of the mythology, just as it was the outer clothing of the Eleusinian and Egyptian mysteries and of hundreds of mythologies all over the world. It may well account for some of the simpler rituals elaborated to fit the mood of the more superstitious sections of the community; but behind it lay a much deeper and more profound view. It took into account not only man's material needs, but his desire to probe the eternal puzzle of his life and its meaning.

Agricultural propitiation ceremonies could never of themselves have developed into the rich symbolism of the plumed serpent or the extra-ordinary idea of the humble, suffering god who was brave enough to save the world from destruction when the sun stood still. The philosophy of sacrifice and of death and rebirth, is on another level entirely. Only from this point of view can any good sense be made of the myths of creation and regeneration that belong to two of the highest ancient cultures in the New World.

Proof of an intentional and psychologically shrewd stratification of ideas can be found in the three different languages used by the Nahua-speaking peoples who inhabited the high central tableland of what today is Mexico. These were the language of the common people, designed to deal with things at an ordinary every-day level; the language of the nobility, more poetic and cultured but with little depth of wisdom; and the language of the magicians or initiates – in more ordinary terms, the priests. This contained in code form every idea an aspiring man might need to achieve true enlightenment.

By analogy with these languages, then, there was a religion of simple agriculture for the profane, one of hierarchies and moral responsibility for the aristocracy, and an esoteric religion of mystery for the initiates. Similarly, every representation of a god or an abstract idea had its corresponding material image, or idol, for the superstitious; a hieroglyph and an associated colour for the noble interested in heraldry, and a mathematical-astronomical-scientific inner symbolism for the priests.

There is nothing unusual in this practice of stratification; it is a feature of many of the great religions of the world and we find it in many forms within Christianity, especially within the Roman Catholic Church where the multiplicity of saints and martyrs, the examples of humanity striving for union with the divine, is attractive to the majority; while the higher meanings of Christ's teaching can be reached by those who make a stronger effort to understand.

The main mythology of the high Mexican tableland was not created by the Aztecs (the heron-people) but by their Nahua-speaking predecessors, including the Toltecs and others farther back. The pre-Hispanic Mexican population was composed of a variety of stock. There were Nahuas on the high central plateau, Olmecs and Totonacs along the Gulf coast, Mixtecs, Zapotecs and Huastecs farther south, Otomies, Tarascans,

The ball court at Copán, showing the stone rings. Ball courts in different forms existed everywhere in old Mexico among all races and cultures. It has never been determined of exactly what the game consisted but the evidence shows that it was much more a rite than a sport. Toltec, tenth to thirteenth centuries A.D.

and Zacatecans in what is today central Mexico, Cora and Huichol Indians to the west, and various nomadic tribes to the north.

Where these various peoples originally came from is uncertain. 'Why were we not simply *here*?' asks the doyen of Mexico's archaeologists, Alfonso Caso. But there have been all manner of theories, including the idea that they came from Asia across the Bering Straits and migrated southward – the opposite theory being that which the Kon-Tiki expedition tried to prove: that migration would have been feasible westward from South America to Polynesia. There is no reason in fact why migrations should not have taken place in both directions at various times in history.

A seventeenth-century Mexican, Sigüenza y Góngora, believed that Quetzalcoatl – the Mexican plumed serpent – was the apostle Thomas and that all the Indians of the New World were descendants of Poseidon, who in his turn was a great-grandson of Noah.

The Indians may have had more than one origin, for they were of many varying physical types and psychological temperaments, and we can see the enormous diversity of the American peoples in their twentieth-century descendants. There are sharp-profiled, hook-nosed Indians typical of the Redskins of nursery tales; others Chinese in feature, with broad, flat cheekbones and the oriental fold of the eyelid. There are regions where the people are stunted, others where they are tall and muscular. Some are fierce and resistant to advances from outsiders or to any suggestion that their old way of life might change; others are more open, gayer, readier to incorporate themselves into modern life. A Mexican novelist, Gregorio López y Fuentes, puts into the mouth of one of his characters in *El Indio* an analysis of some of these differences: 'What is there in common between the Otomí of the central plain, who wards off cold by drinking pulque and sleeping in the ashes, who lives in hovels roofed with maguey chaff and who eats vermin, and the clean Totonac with his brilliant past? What affinity do you find between the taciturn Tepehua and the rough, warlike Huichol?'

This is not quite an accurate description, for the Huichol Indians are decorative and artistic rather than warlike; but it reflects the variety of type that exists today and has always existed in this area popularly thought of as the land of the Aztecs.

The Aztecs, consolidating their power in the area only in the fourteenth century of our era, conquered the peoples occupying what is now a broad area of central Mexico, and became the self-styled successors of the Toltecs (master craftsmen), who had been on the high plateau for several centuries previously. The Toltecs were in their turn relative newcomers, and before their day the other Nahua-speaking people – builders of Teotihuacán and earlier sites – had established the general shape of the mythology.

Farther to the south, and intermingling, was the widespread and older Maya culture centred on what are now Yucatán and Chiapas in Mexico, and the isthmus of Central America. Its early formative period goes back to about 500 B.C.; and its classic period, with its arresting art, ranges from the fourth to the tenth century.

To deal with these cultures separately would entail unnecessary repetition; so they will be discussed together and we shall move from one to another as seems fit, bringing in such modern residues of custom and tradition as may be pertinent, and discussing the beliefs of outlying ancient peoples in so far as they throw light on the two distinct basic cultures: Nahua and Maya.

From very far back there must have been interchange between these two. The great Nahua god Quetzalcoatl includes in his name the shy

A stone model of a pyramid, discovered in the foundations of Moctezuma's palace of Tenochtitlán. At the top the sun is flanked by Huitzilopochtli and Tezcatlipoca, gods of day and night; while on the right side of the stone an eagle alights bearing human hearts. Below this are the gods whose self-sacrifice set the sun in motion. This being a late, Aztec work, all the gods, and the eagle, bear speech-scrolls signifying war. The stone codifies the Aztec belief in war as a way of securing captives, who were then sacrificed and their hearts offered to the sun in repayment for the divine sacrifice. Aztec, *c.* 1500 A.D.

quetzal bird native to the Maya lands. Both cultures have an idea of a holy place which in time became a specific geographical site – the Tollán or Tula of the Nahuas – but which was probably at first the description used for a spiritual condition. The very name Nahua, the name of the linguistic group of people inhabiting the central Mexican plateau, means 'one who speaks with authority', and we shall see how the idea of a chosen people able to speak for the gods was characteristic of Maya and Nahua religion, incomprehensible in many aspects unless we regard it as representing revelation from a high source. Until the end of the nineteenth century at least, and probably down to our own day, the Mayas have believed in diviners called *H'men*, meaning, according to D. G. Brinton, the nineteenth-century investigator, 'those who understand and can do'. Their authority is believed to come from the gods, who give them insight into creation, and power to make cosmic forces work for and not against the well-being of mankind.

At the time of the discovery of America, legends soon circulated of lands where men were giants with supernatural powers, or alternatively pygmies with capacities unknown to ordinary mortals. The legendary races were never discovered, for the simple reason that the powers ascribed to them are the inner ones hinted at in the myths and would not have been visible to those incapable of seeing more than the physical body.

The difficulties standing in the way of a correct understanding of the ancient myths of America are very great, partly because so much was destroyed by the Spaniards, partly because there are signs that the religion had fallen into extreme decay before the Spaniards had even arrived, but mainly because many of the source manuscripts are chronicles written down by Spanish friars who, however laudable their wish to keep a record of dying customs, could not have been expected to be over-sympathetic with what they regarded, not without reason by the time the Spaniards came, as diabolical superstition. Other useful sources are the 'magic books' or indigenous pictograph records, and these are valuable but probably suffer from the degeneration that had overcome the priesthood. The same objection can be made to the few chronicles written by princes of the ancient royal houses after the conquest, on the encouragement of the Spaniards who patronised them.

The compilations made by the friars were written down in indigenous languages, the sounds recorded phonetically as if they had been Spanish. Bernardino de Sahagún, the chief source, was remarkably modern in his

The painted books of Mexico are an important source of information about the lives and beliefs of pre-Hispanic peoples – but few survived the Spaniards, who believed them to be evil. The *Codex Zouche-Nuttall* is a genealogy interspersed with religious myth. The two leaves shown here read from bottom right, where the Lord Nine Ollin is sacrificed at the dedication of a *temazcalli*, a sweating-house for healing disease. (The Lord was dedicated to the sun god as a boy and the sacrifice, on his fifty-second birthday, is voluntary). Above, the body is dressed as an Ocelot Chief and cremated: the torches are carried by two other chiefs, and more bring offerings. In the next leaf, left, Nine Ollin's brother Eight Deer, Lord of Tilantongo, presides at the place of the plumed serpent seated on an ocelot-skin cushion. Below him, his brother's ashes are adorned with feather headdress and turquoise mask and more offerings are brought by two priests. The final cremation is seen on the far left. A quail is sacrificed as a symbol of the sunrise. The symbols above show where it occurred – at Ocelot-Town on Pregnant Mountain of the War Arrow; the day – 6 Ocelot; and year – 10 House, which was probably 1070 A.D. Mixtec, early sixteenth century. British Museum.

Right: a spear thrower. This elaborately carved device gave added leverage to the arm, and it was with weapons like this that the armies of Moctezuma fought Cortés. The carvings represent the noble orders of Eagle and Jaguar. Aztec, sixteenth century.

Ceremonial axeheads were a feature of Mexican ritual and represent some of the finest pre-Hispanic art. This is a very early example, Olmec style.

methods of questioning the Indians, but if there were any priests left who knew the inner meaning of the ancient lore, they would have been unlikely to submit to cross-questioning by foreigners, nor would they have made the true knowledge known to outsiders.

The Indian princes who chose to write their memoirs were in general those who submitted most readily to Spanish education and became Europeanised. The picture books, or magic books, together with wall paintings that belong to the same category, are elaborate codifications to which the keys have sometimes been lost. They consist of symbolic paintings done by the Indians, sometimes at the request of the Spaniards. Their base is either maguey parchment, leather, or cotton; and they are folded in such a way that they can be opened like a screen. They run to about sixteen feet in length, and are around seven inches broad. Some are evidently historical records, others fiction; but the most interesting are mythological and astronomical. The most famous, the *Codex Borgia*, is a description of the Aztec calendar, the gods and their attributes. Another important codex, the Fejervary-Mayer, relates the gods to the calendar.

The most important of the Maya codices are the Dresden, the Paris, and the Tro-Cortesianus. They are written in glyphs that have only recently been deciphered, and they give us some indication of the Maya gods. There are also glyph steles, and the famous wall friezes at Bonampak in the forests of Chiapas. The latter are paralleled in the Nahua culture by the interesting Nahua-Toltec friezes that have been discovered only in recent years in palaces or priestly homes near the pyramids of Teotihuacán.

From these assorted sources we have to do what we can to reconstruct the mythology. By force of circumstances much that can be said remains highly speculative and controversial; but as new investigations are made it becomes clear that surviving sources show us two broad levels of ancient American thought: the superstitious, pantheistic religion of the populace, and the inner religion corresponding in many ways to the Greek and Egyptian mysteries. Both were confounded and their threads intermingled, and both suffered the degeneration that brought with it human sacrifice and other cruelties. But behind the first there seems to have existed a sound native folklore such as peasants in all parts of the world use for their medicinal and agricultural practices; and behind the second a conception of man's true place and purpose in the universe. If the philosophical ideas are fragmentary, we must remember that so too is our evidence. By piecing together the scrambled and coded myths, the fine wall paintings, the codices, and what we know of the etymology of words that enclose philosophical ideas of no little subtlety, we may try to make some plausible guesses about the pre-Hispanic mind.

Lest the reader be put off by the forbidding names, it should be noted that it is quite easy to split these up into component roots or syllables and then to pronounce them phonetically as if the words were Spanish, remembering that the tendency is for the accent to fall on the penultimate, not on the last syllable.

Accents have been omitted from pre-Hispanic names except where these have become assimilated into the post-conquest Spanish-American scene or where they give an indication of the correct pronunciation.

Historical note

To supplement these introductory remarks, the general reader may find it useful to have the myths placed, however sketchily, against their historical background.

Fossils of the so-called Tepexpan man, discovered in 1949 on the edge of an old lake bed on the high Mexican plateau, and some corn cobs that develop from a small, wild variety to the cultivated 'food fit for the gods', suggest that there were human beings in the Americas 6,000 or more years before Christ. The evidence suggests that these early inhabitants were mammoth-hunters, probably nomad, and that they lacked any true culture. However, by 1500 B.C. they had acquired some artistic techniques, and these were practised at Chiapa de Corzo in the Grijalva basin of south-east Mexico – the earliest site that can properly be considered a human settlement.

A later settlement which was found at Tlatilco in the Valley of Mexico, has been dated at about 800 B.C. and has some characteristics that would appear to link it with sites thousands of miles to the south, in Peru. Tlatilco seems to have been connected with the mysterious Olmec culture of the Mexican Gulf, which some research workers think was the original source of Nahua inspiration. Others believe that the culture spread north from the Maya lands.

The Olmec centre at La Venta in the present state of Veracruz was destroyed deliberately and for no known reason between 400 and 300 B.C., leaving Tres Zapotes, to the northwest, to continue whatever cultural tradition the former had contained. These sites belong to a formative period stretching for several centuries on either side of the birth of Christ, by which time there was already the beginning of a culture at Monte Albán outside Oaxaca. Teotihuacán, on the Mexican plateau, is later and appears to have flourished on either side of 300 A.D. From Monte Albán the Zapotec culture spread to nearby Mitla, and from Teotihuacán to Tula, which is almost due north of Mexico City and which is sometimes supposed to have been the capital of the Toltec empire. Other research workers dispute this, and put the centre of the great Toltec culture in Teotihuacán, the site of the great pyramids and many wall paintings which have come to light in what appear to have been palaces or priests' dwellings. There is no doubt that Toltec culture represents the peak of a long development in art and architecture; but the origins of the myths and the religious and philosophical thought probably go back to earlier Nahua-speaking peoples who were their ancestors.

Broadly one may say that two hundred years before Christ a Nahua-speaking culture had been established in the highland valleys of Mexico, and a Maya culture in Yucatán; and that shortly before the birth of Christ the Nahuas and the Mayas both had glyph writing. A century before Christ's birth there were Maya, Zapotec, and Nahua ceremonial centres, which developed into the strong styles seen in Palenque in the Chiapas forest (seventh century), the great temple of Quetzalcoatl in Teotihuacán (eighth century), and the buildings at Copán in Honduras which can be dated about the same time.

The cult of the plumed serpent, with its Buddha-like compassion, was by this time so fully developed that a little later, in the tenth century, the name of the god Quetzalcoatl was adopted by Topiltzin, king of Tula, the last king of the Toltecs whose empire extended down into Yucatán. By this time the Maya cities had passed their greatest period; and about the eleventh century began a decline, precipitated by invasions from the north. But they were still spreading northward in the thirteenth century, trading along the Gulf from Panama to Tampico, about the time when the Aztecs were completing their long migration southward and beginning to settle in the Valley of Anáhuac in the centre of Mexico.

It was not until 1325 that the Aztecs finally occupied islands on the lake of the Mexican plateau and founded their capital, Tenochtitlán, which

17

was finally destroyed by Hernán Cortés in 1519. The conqueror's task was made easier by two facts. First, the surrounding peoples were on his side: they hated their Aztec overlords, with their cruel and bloodthirsty excesses, and sided with the Europeans against them. There was also a pall of dread hanging over the Aztecs; the last Emperor Moctezuma was superstitious and believed that Cortés was the god Quetzalcoatl returned – as it was predicted, in that very year – to reclaim his former lands and people. The Aztecs, proud conquerors for a period of two or three centuries, who had taken over the native language, religion, and art and tried to act as if it were their own, were no longer in a state to defend themselves. It is true that Cortés was soon seen to be anything but a returning god, even by Moctezuma, and his son-in-law Cuauhtémoc fought bravely on when the main Aztec armies had capitulated. But for the Aztecs the end of their world had come.

The Yucatecan Mayas held out against the Spaniards until much later. Montejo the younger, the conqueror of Yucatán, was not able to build his capital, Mérida, until 1542, and resistance from the Mayas continued at least until 1546. Even as late as 1622 the Mayas were holding out in the Itzá centre of Petén in Guatemala, and the last Itzá chief was not put to death until 1697. The Itzás themselves may have come from the Mexican Gulf area but were Maya-speaking. They had, however, a close connection with the Toltecs, with whose help they had been able, during the tenth century, to impose their dominion over a large part of Yucatán. The famous sacrificial well at Chichén, their centre, was probably not a place

of human slaughter but of symbolic sacrifice to the gods. Recent exploration of the well has revealed hundreds of tiny rubber dolls which were probably propitiating images thrown down during certain ceremonies.

There were, then, a number of successive Nahua-speaking cultures extending from the early Nahuas, through the Olmecs and the Toltecs, to the Aztecs; and a number of interrelated Maya cultures that at one time or another mingled with the Nahuas. Sandwiched between, and probably a result of mingling, were the Zapotecs of the Mexican isthmus, and the Huastecs who extended along the Mexican Gulf northward from the Yucatán region which is supposed to have been the original home of the Maya Itzá.

One unexplained mystery befuddles modern scholars: how is it that the New World before the arrival of the Spaniards contained ethnic types of such a wide diversity that there have been clay and stone portraits discovered representing practically every known human race? Alexander von Wuthenau, a German art historian who has lived for many years in Mexico and has studied the ancient cultures, has collected an astonishing variety of portraits.

Where did so many different peoples come from? What exchanges were there, before Columbus, between Mexico and Central America on one side of the Atlantic, and Africa and Europe on the other? Between the New World and the Far East? The legends we shall study have traces of oriental influence, and possibly even of Judaism and Mediterranean cultures. One thing is certain: they are older than the sacrifices, and wiser.

Above and bottom left: Mexico and Central America were peopled by races of very diverse aspect, as the illustrations on the succeeding pages will show. Faces modelled during the Totonac culture of the Veracruz region are very European, while there is a distinctly negroid cast to the colossal Olmec heads at La Venta. In striking contrast are two others shown here: on the left is a pre-classic Maya face from Palenque, and above a Zapotec head from Monte Albán.

Top left: the deep limestone pools, called *cenotes*, were the only steady source of water in Yucatán, a region without rivers. The sacred well at Chichén Itzá is surrounded by vertical cliffs sixty-five feet high and offerings were thrown into the water. Originally these were simple votive offerings of clay and rubber; later ceremonies were elaborate, with offerings of gold and jewels. Recent underwater exploration has revealed no sign that human sacrifices, as described by the Spanish friars, took place in this well.

Tonatiuh, the sun god. His heaven was originally the highest, a place for those who had achieved fulfilment on earth, but the Aztecs made it the abode of warriors. Aztec relief, c. 1500.

TIME AND ETERNITY

'Where there was neither heaven nor earth sounded the first word of God. And He unloosed Himself from His stone, and declared His divinity And all the vastness of eternity shuddered. And His word was a measure of grace, and He broke and pierced the backbone of the mountains. Who was born there? Who? Father, Thou knowest: He who was tender in Heaven came into Being.'

These words from the Maya collection of sacred books, the *Chilam Balam of Chumayel*, set the tone for the myths of creation both of the Maya and Nahua peoples. Unequivocally they affirm a monotheistic doctrine and the timeless quality of the great deity who created the universe. The unknown Maya writer of this *Book of Spirits*, or *Book of the Tiger Priests*, speaks not of *when* there was neither heaven nor earth, but of *where*. He is speaking of a *place* beyond time – not merely of a period when time was not. In Maya terminology this is the 'first time' outside material creation; so that the god-above-all had to descend into the 'second time' before he could declare his divinity. To whom otherwise would he declare it except to himself, the total uncreated essence of all things? The Mayas envisaged an end when creation would return to its beginnings.

'All moons, all years, all days, all winds, reach their completion and pass away. So does all blood reach its place of quiet, as it reaches its power and its throne. Measured was the time in which they could praise the splendour of the Trinity. Measured was the time in which they could know the Sun's benevolence. Measured was the time in which the grid of the stars would look down upon them; and through it, keeping watch over their safety, the gods trapped within the stars would contemplate them.'

This quotation, taken in its context, may be thought to refer to the coming of the Spaniards and the passing of Maya civilisation specifically; but the words reach far beyond any particular time and place and, taken in conjunction with the earlier quotation, reveal the great cyclical concept embodied in the Maya calendar. The Mayas counted not only in days, months, and years, but also in larger periods of time known as *katun* (twenty years), *baktun* (400 years), *pictun* (8,000 years), *calabtun* (158,000 years), and *kincultun* (about 3 million years). The root word *tun* means a stone.

Thus, within the moving procession of the eternal heavens extending to three million years the Mayas felt a stillness, an immobility, something like the immobility of a spoked wheel, which when it is whirled at great speed appears solid and at rest. Everything must turn in its cycle, 'reach completion', and find its quiet place, its 'power' and its 'throne' – in other words its fulfilment and its beginning.

The reference to the Trinity in this quotation may be an interpolation, for the *Chilam Balam* was written down after the Spanish conquest and contains some obvious insertions from Christianity. Nevertheless the fact that the Mayas could so quickly accept a Christian doctrine suggests that it was not incompatible with their own religion. As we shall see later, there were a number of parallels between Maya and Christian thought, including the symbolism of the cross and the idea of death and resurrection.

It is interesting to note in this quotation the reference to the gods 'trapped within the stars'. The supreme god was free, but the forces governing the universe and represented by lesser gods were subject to the laws of time and the revolutions of the heavenly bodies. Freedom was thus relative and depended on the exact position of any particular god in the heavenly hierarchy. Some gods might be aloof from the long, cyclic procession of all created bodies; others would be inside it, fulfilling their duties in smaller cycles perhaps of single galaxies or suns.

An important Maya and Nahua symbol, suggesting a perpetual moving outward to the four points of the created world and inward to a still hub, is the quincunx. This figure is really a cross with its central intersection and the points of its four arms emphasised. Various versions of it occur on pottery, on wall paintings, on the insignia of gods, and carved into temple walls. It had many different interpretations. The Mayas, for instance, had always four *balam* (jaguars or high priests) who stood at the four points of the compass and are still believed to stand invisibly on guard. Together with time, space is thus given a special and miraculous significance. Like the 'first time' outside material creation, there must have been a 'first space'. Indeed the two concepts cannot be separated. Space-time does not of necessity exist. On the highest possible level it merges into the absolute being of the all–powerful god. At any moment since the beginning of creation it might – to the consternation of all living things – have fallen apart. The *balam*, the guardians, hold it together.

Each of the cardinal points of the compass had for the ancients its own

A stone arrow, probably a votive offering to the god of war Huitzilopochtli. Arrows were important symbols to the Aztecs, and in one ceremony they were cast to the four quarters. Fourteenth to sixteenth centuries A.D.

colour: red for the east where the sun rises, white for the north where all is cold, black for the west where the sun sets in darkness, and yellow for the golden warmth of the south. At each point stood a sacred ceiba (silk-cotton) tree, fertilising and feeding life in the four directions. Each tree had its colour, and in each tree nested a bird. It seems, too, that there must have been a central tree, green in colour to represent the fountain of all life.

The position of the colours is not always constant, and the Nahuas often associated yellow with the east, white with the north, black with the west, and red with the south. One gets the impression of a revolving sequence, possibly (though this is speculation) associated with changes in the relative positions of astral bodies.

There is a Nahua poem describing a ritual turning to the four quarters. In this symbolic chant the east is called 'the place where the light emerges' and the eagle, tiger, serpent, rabbit and deer who live there are yellow in colour. South is called 'the place where death comes' and the colour of its creatures is red. West is 'the region of the holy seed ground' and its colour is white. North is 'the land of thorns' and its colour is blue. As the initiate hurls his arrows first in one direction and then in another, he attains to the gods. Finally he places his arrows in the hands of the Old God, the god of Time, who rules over all the cardinal points.

The assertion that the west and not the east is the seed ground suggests a perpetual recreation of life out of death, or at least disappearance in the phenomenal world, and rebirth when light dawns in the east on the following day. As the sun dies or disappears, the seed for its revival is planted.

One of the most important Maya scholars, Sylvanus Morley, notes that the peasants of Guatemala still use symbolic colours in their weaves, black representing war weapons because it is the colour of obsidian; yellow, maize or food; red, for obvious reasons, blood; and blue, sacrifice. Green is a symbol of royalty because the green quetzal feathers were the insignia of kings.

In one ceremony persisting to this day, old colour meanings are transferred to Christianity. Red is east or St Dominic the teacher; north white or St Gabriel of the last judgement; black west or St James the younger; and yellow south or Mary Magdalene – here representing fertility. There seems no reason why these particular figures should have been selected but they have apparently come to stand in the modern Maya mind for the *balam* of old.

In pre-Hispanic times Maya youths painted themselves black until the time came for them to marry, when they changed to red. But black was always used to represent fasting. Prisoners were striped black and white, and priests were painted blue. Throughout ancient Mexico and Central America the colour red was associated with death or mourning. Bones were sometimes painted red, and tombs were frequently stained with a brick-coloured dye.

Steps to heaven and hell

The whole world was supposed to rest on the back of a crocodile – or perhaps four crocodiles corresponding to the four compass points; and these in turn floated on a lake.

From a flat cross-section of the world represented by the cardinal points and diverse colours, there rose a ladder of thirteen rungs leading to heaven; and another leading downward by nine steps to hell. The steps on the ladders are not always consistently named in the various documents, but broadly speaking the topmost rung of the heavenly ladder was occu-

Left: the rain god in his heaven, a light-hearted place of flowers, songs and butterflies. Tlaloc presides, attended by priests, and water flows from his hands while water creatures play at his feet. The happy souls are seen in the lower half. Reconstructed wall painting from Tepantitla. Teotihuacán culture, first to sixth centuries A.D.

Far left: jade plaque found near Puerto Barrientos, Guatemala. It is from this, the oldest dated Maya object, that archaeologists date Maya history. The obverse (above) shows the planet Venus, who was the god Kukulcan. The reverse (below) shows a number of glyphs which give a date according to the Maya calendar, totalling 94,537 days from the beginning of the Maya era. This corresponds to roughly 320 A.D.

Below: a decorated clay cup from Villahermosa in the state of Tabasco.

pied by the dual god-goddess who is Ometeotl, 'god of the near and close', 'he who is at the centre' or 'within the ring', he to whom we owe the existence of life, self-inventing, self-creating, lord of all Heaven and Earth and even of the Land of the Dead.

The duality of this god was a duality in quality. It stood for the negative and positive, male and female principles in the universe, light and shadow, yes and no. It was not a duality arising from polytheism. The concept was monotheistic and represented the equilibrium rather than the diversity within creation.

The next four steps below the land of Ometeotl are mysterious. Nobody knows more about them than the mere fact that they existed, though the one immediately below Ometeotl was sometimes said to be the abode of innocent children. It is as if these received some special blessing or shelter from the god above all.

Then came a land of tempests and of multiple gods. It would seem that here for the first time strife entered the universe, dividing Ometeotl into his many facets.

Immediately below were two rungs of the ladder belonging to night and day, or to dust and air. Then came a land of shooting stars or fiery snakes; then of birds and of the planet Venus; and, rather curiously below Venus, a place occupied by the Sun and the four hundred warriors created by Tezcatlipoca. Farther below these was the Milky Way, pictured as a female skeleton. The lowest of the rungs in heaven was the land of moon and clouds.

Entwined serpents, on a Classic Maya bowl, representing Time. British Museum.

Right: the Toltec culture flourished at Tula, where these colossal figures once supported the entrance of the temple of Tlahuixcalpantecuhtli, Lord of the House of Dawn – Quetzalcoatl as the morning star. This god was also the culture hero of the Toltecs, who dominated southern Mexico before the coming of the Aztecs and whose influence on the Maya culture is plainly discernible. Eighth to twelfth centuries A.D.

TIME AND ETERNITY

Twelve rungs may have been paired, with the thirteenth forming the apex. The nine rungs below the earth would then also have been paired in four steps with a lower pole forming the infernal regions. This pairing no doubt represented the dual nature of matter, growing in its negative and positive aspects ever more rarified and luminous until it found unity in heaven, and ever denser and colder until it descended to the heaviest, lowest point of creation in hell. (The discrepancies between the true cosmic placing of the Sun, planets and Milky Way may be due to a distorted record. We can hardly suppose that people with so accurate a calendar were ignorant of the general positions of the heavenly bodies.)

The nine steps down to hell seem to us more cohesive. First the soul arrived at a river guarded by a yellow dog. Then it had to pass between two mountain peaks, in order to reach one of pure obsidian. Lower still it met bitter winds, then banners, then arrows, then a wild beast. Near the end of its journey it passed through a narrow place, and finally the soul found itself at rest and at peace.

But hell and the lower steps should not be thought of entirely as places to which the wicked went as a punishment (reference to hell as a place for the wicked may be an imposition from orthodox Christianity). Hell was regarded as a necessary point of transition in the circular journey of all created things. These must, by an inevitable cosmic process, plunge into matter and rise again to reach the light. The process takes place in time, and time is important as being the vehicle of man's pilgrimage through material creation and back to his maker. As the sun disappears in the west, the seeds of its rebirth are planted.

The thirteen steps to heaven and the nine to the lower regions should not be confused with three different heavens to which the Nahua dead were supposed to go. The first and lowest of these was Tlalocan, Land of Water and Mist: a kind of paradise where happiness was of a very earthly variety but purer and less changeable. Here men played leapfrog and chased butterflies and sang songs. One fresco from Teotihuacán depicts this scene in a charmingly light-hearted manner. It is a sensual world for the gourmet with discernment. Happiness is conceived of in a simple-minded and materialistic way. The great authority on the ancient Mexicans, Fray Bernardino de Sahagún, says that in this land there was a perpetual abundance of maize, pumpkins, green peppers, tomatoes, beans, and flowers. Tlaloques, benign little mannikins employed by Tlaloc the rain god, are ministers of this paradise of plenty, which is a place of rebirth. It is supposed that after four years of sojourn here, souls return once more to mortal life. Unless we can reach higher, the perpetual round goes on. Most people on earth are probably destined to perpetuate this cycle of birth on earth, death into Tlalocan, and rebirth on earth. Their desires and their pleasures never rise above the simple pursuits depicted in the fresco.

But there was also Tlillan-Tlapallan, the land of the black and the red (black and red in conjunction signify wisdom). This was the paradise of the initiates who had found a practical application for the teaching of the god-king Quetzalcoatl. It was the land of the fleshless, the place where people went who had learned to live outside their physical bodies or, it would be better to say, unattached to them; a place celebrated in many ancient poems and greatly to be desired.

Farther beyond was Tonatiuhican, land of Tonatiuh, House of the Sun, often misrepresented as a military-political abode of warriors; but this is only because the Nahua 'holy war' has been wrongly interpreted as an earthly war against earthly enemies. The third paradise was probably

reserved for those who had achieved full illumination in the quest for deserved and eternal happiness.

So we have a series of three paradises, each more perfect than the one below and to be attained only by ever more intense spiritualisation and sacrifice of the gross physical world. Men whose desires were for good food and gaiety would go to the Land of Water and Mist, and then return to earth. Those who had acquired some kind of immortality apart from the perishable body would aspire to the Land of the Fleshless. And those who achieved still higher perfection might become worthy of living in the House of the Sun.

One's fate might of course be bad, causing one to go after death to the inferno called Mictlán – a dark place ruled over by the god Mictlantecuhtli and his consort Mictlancihuatl. This place was at the centre of the earth, and much less desirable than the cloudlands of the warrior souls. Nevertheless souls there did not suffer. They merely endured a rather colourless existence – perhaps the worst fate of all.

The great earth monster

Before the various paradises existed, the primordial substance seems to have been water. In a Nahua creation myth the great female Earth Monster, with innumerable mouths, swam in the formless waters devouring all she saw. When the gods Quetzalcoatl and Tezcatlipoca (whom we shall study later in more detail) saw how things were they determined that the Earth must acquire form. They changed themselves into two serpents. The first seized the Earth Monster by the right hand and the left foot. The other seized the left hand and the right foot. Together they grappled until the Monster broke in two. Her lower part rose to form the heavens, and her upper half descended to become the Earth. 'As above, so below. As in Heaven, so on Earth'. The entwined serpents are Time itself; and even today there are surviving beliefs suggesting that time was never thought of apart from space. The Nahuas could envisage only a space-time continuum – and the breaking up of the Earth Monster to form heaven and earth is a description of the origins of the linked space-time continuum in the material world.

The Earth Monster is the goddess, says the myth, who sometimes weeps at night, longing to eat human hearts, and she refuses to remain silent so long as she is not fed, and she will not bear fruit unless she is sprinkled with human blood. Life must be sacrificed to the great creature who nurtures life: a simple truth later distorted by the Aztecs who made it a pretext for sacrificing the hearts of their enemies. All living matter returns to earth. Ashes to ashes, dust to dust. But Earth sustains us too, and this the Nahua gods acknowledged after they had dismembered her, by allowing her to produce things necessary to man's well-being. Her hair became long grass and trees and flowers; her skin the lawns and the flowers with which they are studded like jewels. Her eyes became little caverns, wells, and fountains; her mouths, great caves for man's shelter; and her nose, hills and valleys.

Chiapas Indians, descendants of pre-Hispanic peoples, still use the same kind of graphic illustration, as when they say that the rainbow is a wall created to stop the passage of rain, or that the rivers are made with a great plough driving furrows through the land.

Stories of transubstantiation

One wide-ranging creation myth, which explains a series of phenomena from the birth of stars to the appearance of humans on earth, begins

The Lord of the Region of Death, Totonac style; sixth to ninth centuries A.D. Mictlantecuhtli (bottom) ruled over a nether world where there was neither pain nor pleasure, just a dreary eternal existence. The figure of his consort Mictlancihuatl is Aztec, a stone carving from a later period.

with the existence in some heaven of the dual pair Ometeotl, sometimes called Ometecuhtli or Citlaltonac and his consort Omecihuatl or Citlalinicue.

One day the goddess gave birth to a knife of hard stone which she threw to earth, and 1,600 heroes were born. They were alone (man having died in one of the not infrequent calamities that wiped all living things from the face of the earth). These heroes sent an ambassador to their mother asking her to create men who would serve them. Their mother sent a hawk with the message that if their thoughts could be made nobler they would be worthy to live with her eternally in heaven. Not being of a highly spiritual or ambitious turn of mind, the heroes decided that they would prefer to live on earth. So they went to the god of the underworld and asked him to provide them with either a bone or the ashes of past men. These they would sprinkle with their own blood, and from them would issue a man and a woman who would multiply and repopulate the earth. Quetzalcoatl's twin Xolotl went to the underworld and brought back the bone. But the god of the underworld pursued him in anger. Xolotl fell with his bone, which broke into unequal parts. However, he managed to reach the brothers, who sprinkled it with their own blood. Four days later a male child was born, and three days after that a female. Xolotl raised the human pair on the milk of the thistle, and thus humankind was reborn to life on earth.

We see in this story how impossible it is for mankind to exist without some principle entering the human flesh from above. In this case the principle is represented by the blood of the 1,600 heroes, the life-substance of the stars in the Milky Way.

A gold lip-plug in the form of a serpent with a bifid tongue. The serpent symbolised many things to the peoples of pre-Hispanic Mexico, but particularly strength (through Xincoatl) and wisdom (through Quetzalcoatl). It was also a symbol of both earth and time. In the form of serpents Tezcatlipoca and Quetzalcoatl subdued the Earth Monster, who broke into two parts to become Earth and Heaven. Mixtec culture, eighth to eleventh centuries A.D.

In another story the gods descended into a cave in which a prince was lying with the goddess called Precious Flower. From their union was born a god-child called the Well-Beloved, who immediately died and was buried. Out of the ground, from his body, there sprang many of the plants that were to supply man's basic needs. From his hair grew cotton; from his ears, seed-bearing plants; from his nostrils, a herb which is good for cooling fevers; from his fingers, the sweet potato; from his fingernails, maize; and so on until he had produced about a thousand varieties of fruits and grain.

On one level the god-child is a material symbol of fertility; on another he represents death and rebirth, just as the Egyptian and Greek mysteries did. In the Nahua myth, however, the equivalent of Persephone came not from the underworld but from above. Even if the stuff of plants and herbs sprang from the buried body of the god-child, life could never have been sustained without an activating principle of a higher order. So it occurred to the wind god that it is well enough for man to rejoice in the fruits of the earth, but he must have love too. It occurred to him, then, to go in search of the maiden Mayahuel, whom he found in the company of many others, all asleep, in the charge of an ancient guardian called Tzitzimitl.

The wind god bestirred Mayahuel, who awakened and agreed to go with him to earth. Thus the dormant force of love was roused and made active by the wind god. As the pair touched ground, they shot up into a beautiful tree with two great branches. One was known as the Precious Willow and belonged to the wind god. The other – the flowering branch – was the maiden's.

In the meantime old Tzitzimitl had awakened. Discovering that Mayahuel was no longer with her she became very angry. Tzitzimitl evidently represents the forces in nature that have a vested interest in inertia, passivity, and sleep. It did not suit her that love should be awakened and breathed into life by the wind. With an army of young gods who were her henchmen she descended to earth, and there discovered the tree which she immediately caused to split in two. In the flowering branch the old woman recognised the characteristics of Mayahuel. She shared out bits of it among the gods, who devoured them ravenously. The other branch, belonging to the wind god, remained untouched.

When the invaders had returned to their abode in heaven, the wind god changed himself back into his rightful shape, gathered together the bones of the maiden, and buried them in the fields. From them sprang a plant which produced white wine for men.

The story of Mayahuel is the story of the transubstantiation of matter; and the emphasis is on a fusion of heavenly and earthly ingredients. Neither can do without the other. Inertia, or earth, will remain with its possibilities unfulfilled if love – coming from above – does not infuse it with life. But neither can the higher powers work except through the stuff of the dead tree. Matter is the prop and stay of spirit.

The same theme recurs in a story which tells how one day the Sun shot an arrow which split open a rock. From within it were born a man and a woman. They were incomplete, possessing only head and thorax but lacking their lower limbs. They hopped over the ground like sparrows; and only when they had united in a kiss of love were they able to give birth to a complete man, father of mankind. It is interesting here that mankind exists in spirit (in his upper parts), but it is only when he is awakened by love that he becomes incarnate in an earthly form.

Between heaven and earth there must be a bridge; and this is formed

The wind god Ehecatl, a manifestation of Quetzalcoatl. He brought love to mankind when he bestirred the maiden Mayahuel. Their love was made manifest by a beautiful tree which grew up where they alighted on earth. Aztec sculpture, fourteenth to sixteenth centuries A.D.

Detail of the rim of the stone of Tizoc, who became
ruler of the Aztecs in 1481. A sacrificial stone,
there was a depression in the centre which received
human hearts. It was two and a half feet thick and
eight feet in diameter, and carved with scenes
commemorating the monarch's deeds. Victorious
Aztec warriors can be seen leading their captives by
the hair.

Right: the old fire god Huehueteotl. One of the oldest deities of ancient America, his ceremonies were particularly important at the conclusion of each fifty-two year cycle of time, when old fires were quenched and new ones lighted to keep time moving. Pottery figure from Cerro de las Mesas, Veracruz.

Below: a Zapotec representation of the bat god, the adversary of the valiant twins in the *Popol Vuh* story.

by the gods. After one creation, for example, the Goddess of the Jade Petticoat caused it to rain so hard that all human beings were changed into fishes. Then the gods decided that the heavens must be held up by four giant figures called Falling Eagle; Serpent of Obsidian Knives; Resurrection; and Thorny Flowers. Quetzalcoatl and Tezcatlipoca also helped to prop up the heavens, the former becoming a Precious Tree, and the latter a Tree of Mirrors.

It is difficult to be sure what the four pillars supporting heaven represent; but it would appear that the Falling Eagle symbolises the descent of a heavenly and activating principle into earth; and that the Serpent of Obsidian Knives is a principle of sacrifice needed for the process of incarnation, whose perpetual cycle cannot be escaped except through Resurrection and the growth of flowers. But even flowers have thorns, for nothing in creation can avoid the dual quality of matter with its beauty and its suffering. In the same way the wind god, an aspect of Quetzalcoatl, represents spirit freed from matter, while the god of the smoking mirror, Tezcatlipoca, is the phenomenal world.

How music was made

Tezcatlipoca besought Quetzalcoatl that he should make the journey to the House of the Sun, from which all life comes. He gave Quetzalcoatl specific instructions: that when he reached the seashore he must enlist the help of Tezcatlipoca's three servants who were called Cane and Conch, Water Woman, and Water Monster. Quetzalcoatl was to order these

Left: Chalchihuitlicue, goddess of the Jade Petticoat. In one creation she provided the bridge to heaven, without which mankind cannot exist, by using her power as the consort of the rain god. She caused a downpour that covered the earth, and turned men into fishes that they might use the water as a passage. Pottery figure from Tajín, fourth to ninth centuries A.D.

Below: a clay figure from the early Olmec culture. The kneeling figure is wearing a beast's skin, and is probably an early example of one of the cults which later became the knightly orders.

three to entwine together to form a bridge over which he could pass to reach the Sun. On arriving at the Sun he was to ask for musicians, and was to bring them back to earth to delight the souls of men.

Quetzalcoatl did as he was told, and when the Sun saw him approaching he warned his musicians not to utter a word. Any who opened his mouth would have to return to earth with the wind god. The musicians, clad in white, red, yellow, and green, resisted the temptation to unloose their tongues; but at last one of them relented, gave voice, and descended with Quetzalcoatl to earth where he was able to give mankind the pleasure of music.

In a sixteenth-century Nahua manuscript there is a poem describing this incident:

Tezcatlipoca – god of heaven
and of the four quarters of the heavens –
came to earth and was sad.
He cried from the uttermost depths of the four quarters:
   'Come, O wind!
   Come, O wind!
   Come, O wind!
   Come, O wind!'
The querulous wind, scattered over earth's sad bosom,
rose higher than all things made;
and, whipping the waters of the oceans

Quetzalcoatl (spirit) dances before Tezcatlipoca (matter); a page from the *Codex Borbonicus*. The legends of ancient Mexico demonstrate that the worlds of matter and spirit are coexistent and each has something which the other needs.

Right: two great gods at Teotihuacán. The pyramid usually called after the plumed serpent was in fact shared by the rain god Tlaloc, and symbolic representations of the two alternate on the façade of the pyramid. At one time the serpent masks were coloured, with eyes made of obsidian. The temple which surmounted the pyramid no longer exists.

and the manes of the trees,
arrived at the feet of the god of heaven.
There he rested his black wings
and laid aside his endless sorrow.
Then spoke Tezcatlipoca:
    'Wind, the earth is sick from silence.
    Though we possess light and colour and fruit,
    yet we have no music.
    We must bestow music upon all creation.
    To the awakening dawn,
    to the dreaming man,
    to the waiting mother,
    to the passing water and the flying bird,
    life should be all music!
    Go then through the boundless sadness
    between the blue smoke and the spaces
    to the high House of the Sun.
    There the father Sun is surrounded
    by makers of music
    who blow their flutes sweetly
    and, with their burning choir,
    scatter light abroad.
    Go, bring back to earth a cluster – the most flowering –
    of those musicians and singers.'
Wind traversed the earth that was plunged in silence
and trod with his strength of breath pursued,
till he reached the heavenly roof of the World
where all melodies lived in a nest of light.
The Sun's musicians were clad in four colours.
White were those of the cradle songs;
red those of the epics of love and of war;

A gold disk representing the sun. It was to the House of the Sun that Quetzalcoatl journeyed – at the behest of Tezcatlipoca – in search of music to gladden the heart of man. Mixtec culture.

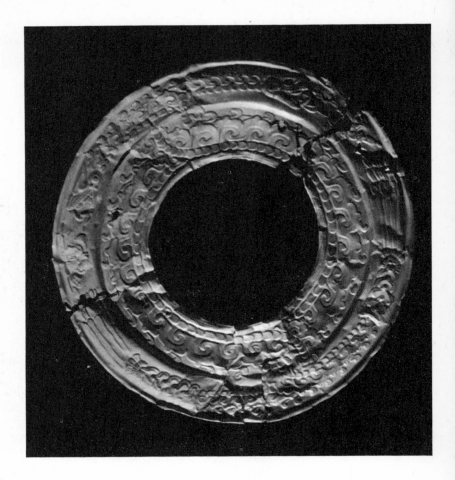

A cast gold pendant from Veraguas, Panama. The upper end shows a jaguar, the lower a crocodile.

sky blue the troubadours of wandering cloud;
yellow the flute players enjoying gold
milled by the Sun from the peaks of the World.
There were no musicians the colour of darkness.
All shone translucent and happy, their gaze turned forward.
When the Sun saw the wind approaching he told his musicians:
    'Here comes the bothersome
    wind of earth:
    Stay your music!
    Cease your singing!
    Answer him not!
    Whoever does so
    will have to follow him
    back down there into silence.'
From the stairways of light
of the House of the Sun,
Wind with his dark voice shouted:
    'Come, O musicians!'
None replied.
The clawing wind raised his voice and cried:
    'Musicians, singers!
    The supreme Lord of the World is calling you...!'
Now the musicians were silent colours;
they were a circling dance held fast
in the blinding flame of the Sun.
Then the god – he of the heaven's four quarters –
waxed wroth.
From the remotest places,

whipped by his lightning lash,
flocks of cloud whose blackened wombs
were stabbed and torn by lightning
assembled to besiege the House of the Sun.
His bottomless throat let loose the thunder's roar.
Everything seemed to fall flat in a circle
beneath the World's mad roof, in whose breast
the Sun like a red beast drowned.
Spurred on by fear,
the musicians and singers then ran for shelter
to the wind's lap.
Bearing them gently
lest he should harm their tender melodies,
the wind with that tumult of happiness in his arms
set out on his downward journey, generous and contented.
Below, Earth raised its wide dark eyes to heaven
and its great face shone, and it smiled.
As the arms of the trees were uplifted,
there greeted the wind's wanderers
the awakened voice of its people,
the wings of the quetzal birds,
the face of the flowers
and the cheeks of the fruit.
When all that flutter of happiness landed on earth,
and the Sun's musicians spread to the four quarters,
then Wind ceased his complaining and sang,
caressing the valleys, the forests and seas.
Thus was music born on the bosom of earth.

Monte Albán, general view. One of the most spectacular cities of pre-Hispanic Mexico and one of the oldest.

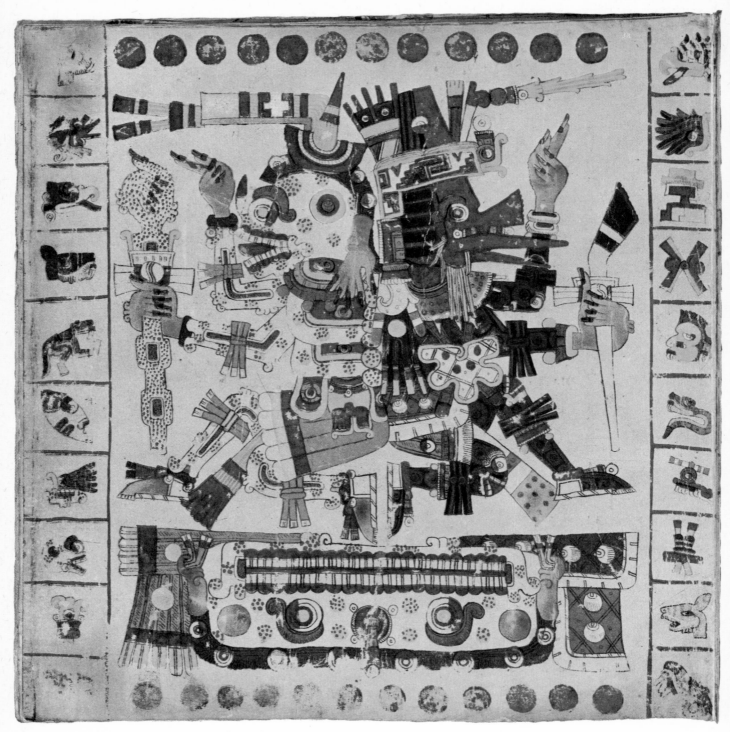

The plumed serpent seen as a performer of miracles.
In his manifestation as the wind god Ehecatl, he
breathes life into a skeleton figure representing the
god of death Mictlantecuhtli. *Codex Borgia.*

The strangely shaped structure at Calixtlahuaca was dedicated to the wind god Ehecatl and recognises his ability to pass where he will.

Thus did all things learn to sing:
the awakening dawn,
the dreaming man,
the waiting mother,
the passing water and the flying bird.
Life was all music from that time on.

Once again, throughout this myth, we notice that matter, the noumenal world, and spirit, the phenomenal, must always be closely intertwined. It even appears that in some cases the phenomenal world rules over the noumenal and Tezcatlipoca has the right to give orders to Quetzalcoatl. There is really no vertical hierarchy here, but only a godly kind of peaceful coexistence, or rather a mutual self-help society in which the noumenal and the phenomenal exchange strength and music, to form the miracle of spirit incarnate.

'Indian time'

The belief that the noumenal and phenomenal worlds were continually interacting one upon the other was probably in part responsible for the attitude toward time natural to all pre-Hispanic peoples and to their descendants today. Workers among modern American Indian communities have noted that the pure indigenous peoples – as distinct from the so-called *ladinos* who have adopted western customs – live in a space-time quite different from ours. It is not just that they are more leisurely, less rushed, and of course totally unaware of clocks. It is rather that – in spite of Einstein, modern nuclear physics, and those events that might by now have been expected to upset our purely sense-based view of time – we continue to think of yesterday, today, and tomorrow as proceeding in a single line and always in one direction. It could be said that our time is horizontal. Indian time, on the other hand, is a completely different conception. It is vertical and static. It moves to no particular appointment in the future. Future and past are extraordinarily confused in the Indian mind, and even the concept of velocity is difficult to grasp, as it was to a Oaxacan Indian who once told me that it would take an hour for me to reach a certain village; and, he added after some thought, 'Two hours if you walk quickly enough.' It is easier for the Indian to describe time in relation to growth or change that is visible, as when peasants measure the distance from village to village in terms of 'a hat and a half' or 'two hats', according to the time it takes to plait the straw as they walk.

To the American Indian the past is not gone forever but is still present somewhere, as it is in the result – the hat – of the handiwork undertaken while walking. The Indians were, however, acutely aware that time, like all else in the universe, is mortal. Fires must be lighted every fifty-two years to keep it going. But the mainspring of this fifty-two year clock (in the old days it had to be wound up by prayers and bonfires) was a cyclical one.

At the end of the fifty-two-year period the fires were put out everywhere in the land. The wooden and stone statues of gods were cast into the water, together with pestles and hearth stones. Homes were swept clean and all rubbish thrown away. At midnight, when time had run out, the Aztecs would kindle a new fire on the breast of a captive, chosen for his noble birth. The captive's heart fed the fire, and if there was not a sufficient blaze it was supposed that the sun would be extinguished and the demons of darkness would descend to devour man, or men might be changed into beasts. Women at this time were held in fear, locked in the granaries and made to wear masks of maguey leaves. Children were also masked, and were kept awake with cuffs and kicks in case they should slumber off and be turned into mice. Everyone waited expectantly for dawn and rejoiced when it finally came, pricking their ears and sprinkling blood on the fire. From the main fire a flame was taken by relays of runners to every temple in the land. Men and women rejoiced at the promise of new life. They put on new garments, redecorated their houses, made new vessels for the rituals, renovated the temples; sacrifices were offered of incense and quail, and amaranth seed cakes were eaten with honey; but nobody was allowed to drink between daybreak and noon. As noon approached, captives were ceremonially bathed and then sacrificed, grains of maize cooked on their fires being distributed to all the people to eat.

The symbol of the cross was known to ancient Americans, who seem to have regarded the horizontal arm as signifying the transitory and the perishable, the vertical one as the eternal and the stable. The vertical arm represented time in the various heavens and underworlds, whereas the horizontal direction was associated with the passage of the sun across the sky.

All the great architectural monuments of Mexico and Central America – Teotihuacán, Tajín, Monte Albán, Mitla, Palenque, Bonampak, Chichén Itzá, Uxmal, Tulúm, Petén, Copán – are expressions of an eternally recurring space-time. The Aztec habit of building one pyramid on top of another every fifty-two years is a manifestation of this, but so also is the massive horizontal planning of the great courtyards and palaces, and the solid base of the pyramids, rising often fairly sharply to their peaks, but firmly set on the ground as if the architects were determined at all costs that they should endure for ever.

The attitude to time is also shown in doctrines concerning free will and predestination. We have seen how immortality could be of different grades, so that a man might pass to a paradise – the Land of Water and Mist – that closely simulated conditions on earth. If he were able to transcend the body, he might continue to the Land of the Fleshless; and thence to full immortality in the House of the Sun. There was a gradual progression from relative darkness to purest light, from earthbound satisfaction to spiritual joy.

A priest of the fire god wearing an elaborate headdress. Pottery figure from Las Remojadas, Veracruz.

MAN-BEAST RELATIONSHIPS

Other beliefs, some of which have been perpetuated to our day, were of a more superstitious nature though they may have arisen from a true appreciation of the close interconnection of man with the rest of organic life. Before studying various man-beast relationships, we should notice how carefully the pre-Hispanic Indians observed the characteristics of living creatures and how talented they were at giving them symbolic meaning. The ancients sculpted, modelled, and painted animals often naturalistically but more frequently in stylized versions to emphasize the qualities or appearances peculiar to each.

Foremost in the precolumbian bestiary was the snake or serpent, definitely associated with Time in the Maya mythology, more obliquely so in the Nahua. Contrasted with the serpent was the quetzal bird, that shy forest dweller capable of releasing man from Time's bondage; and the vulture who was sometimes pictured in mortal combat with the serpent.

The eagle was placed in opposition to the two cat-like animals, the jaguar and the ocelot. In Maya symbolism the jaguar's day was *Ix*, day of obsidian, the day on which heaven and earth embraced. In a Nahua

The serpent columns at Chichén Itzá. In the long shadows the Chac Mool figure watches eternally at the approach to the Temple of the Warriors in the city founded, legend says, by Kukulcan, the Maya Quetzalcoatl.

The interior of the sanctuary of the knightly orders at Malinalco. The alternating figures of eagle and ocelot were in fact seats for the chief dignitaries of the orders. The whole is carved from solid rock. Fourteenth to sixteenth centuries A.D.

story describing the rising and setting of the sun, the eagle stood for the day sun and the ocelot for the star on its night journey through the underworld. Two Nahua orders of knighthood were named after the eagle and the ocelot (the American tiger), and one particularly fine Mexican carving shows a knight-eagle with strangely European features looking out from the visor-headdress representing the bird.

The screech owl and the dog were associated by the Mayas with death and burial. Both Nahuas and Mayas had their equivalents of Cerberus, the Nahua dog being Xolotl and the Maya Pek, dog of lightning. Dogs were the first animals on the continent to be domesticated, and they were held sacred, sometimes being bred for particular characteristics such as hairlessness, which is a feature of the dog called today the Xoloitzcuintli. (This Xoloitzcuintli is not to be confused with that other native domestic Mexican dog, the well-known Chihuahua, popular today in the United States. The Xoloitzcuintli is a larger dog and is believed to be the first animal domesticated in the Americas. The race had almost died out a few years ago, but an English dog-lover, Norman Pelham Wright, was able to find a few pure specimens, and there are now about seventy registered with the Mexican kennel club.)

Snail and tortoise, being the slowest creatures, represented the winter and summer solstice. Another type of snail, the sea mollusc, was one of the most important symbols of death and resurrection because its whorled shape fittingly described the cyclic quality of life, growth, and decay. Butterflies, born out of the caterpillar in the chrysalis, were also

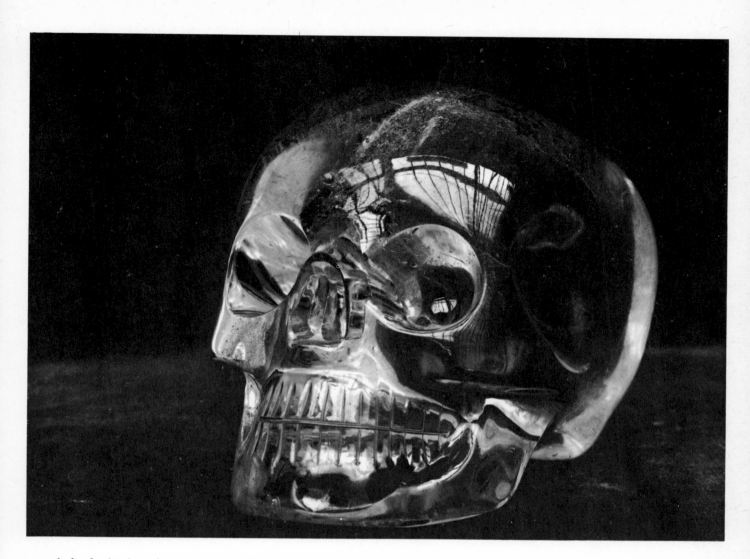

a symbol of rebirth and regeneration, of happiness and joy.

The Mayas told of a bloodthirsty bat called Camazotz, with large teeth and claws and with a nose the shape of a flint knife, who could easily sever a man's head from his body as he once did to the Maya heavenly twins when they were contending against the powers of evil.

There were mysterious Maya ceremonies connected with bees, which seem to have symbolised chosen people of great industry and potential. In Maya symbolism the fish is also common, being sometimes held in the mouth of a heron; so too the frog, the crocodile, the turtle, and other water creatures. These understandably held much less fascination for the Nahuas, who lived far from the coastlands and were more familiar with the turkey (symbol of Tezcatlipoca), the rabbit who was flung in the face of the moon, and other highland fauna.

An awareness of death permeated the life of the Mexicans, and provided the motive for some of their finest art. This skull, carved from rock crystal, is Aztec and dates from the fifteenth century A.D.

Immortality and the soul

The sense of the wholeness and interpenetration of all living things was so strong in the ancient American peoples that they believed a man's fate to be determined by his birthday, and also by his name, which even today is linked with his animal totem. *Naguales* were guardian spirits that took the form of an animal or a bird and presided over a man's fate. A man would receive his particular *nagual* by going into the forest and sleeping among the birds and beasts. There he would either dream of one or, when he wakened, would find himself confronted by his guardian spirit with whom he would be obliged to make a life-long contract. It was

41

supposed that some people had the power of transforming themselves into their *nagual*, in the same way that Gucumatz – one of the heroes of the *Popol Vuh*, could transform himself into a serpent, an eagle, a tiger, and lower forms of life. *Naguals* could become invisible and travel swiftly from place to place.

In modern primitive belief the *nagual* is the first creature to cross the newborn baby's path. Ashes are sprinkled outside the place where the child is born so that the footprints of the animal can be captured and the correct name determined. The animal becomes a kind of second soul to the child, whose physical appearance and psychic features become similar to the *nagual*'s. Some powerful men, for instance, have thunderbolts as *naguals*; others, who seem humble but are really fierce, have a tiger. If a person prays to his *nagual* it will do what he wishes, but he must know how to pray. A man and his *nagual* are not interchangeable, but when a man dies his *nagual* dies, and vice versa.

The identification of the *nagual* with the person can be extended to include almost anything that appears to represent him, and especially his photograph. In many parts even today the peasants fear cameras and turn away from them with the rapidity of a person pursued by death. Something goes out of them, they feel, is diminished, and enters the photographic image. Still worse, if the photograph should fall into the hands of an ill-wisher, damage done to the photograph can be transferred to the subject of it.

The linking of birth and death to the *nagual* is predestination in its most rigid form. It is also alarmingly accidental, for who can tell whether a coyote or a hare, or even – as in one story – a bicycle (animate in Indian thought) might not be the first to cross a baby's path? Nevertheless fate can be changed by courage in the battle of life as well as on the battlefield itself, by fasting and prayers, and above all by creating a heart and a mind worthy of the gods.

The Chontal Indians of Oaxaca say that a man's soul resides in his heart or breath and has a human shape. When people dream of the dead, they are seeing their souls. During a dream the soul leaves the body and goes to meet other souls. Apart from the soul, and less tied to the physical body, man possesses sense or judgment which resides in the head but which can come and go at will. One may, for example, think mentally of a place and inhabit it for a time in imagination.

The Otomí Indians of the central Mexican plain believe that the soul dies with the body, but the Mexicans and the other people of Anáhuac thought it was immortal. Soldiers killed in war or women who died in childbirth went to the House of the Sun, where they lived happily ever after. Every day the soldiers celebrated the Sun's birth by following it to its zenith, where they were met by the women who led the Sun to its decline in the west. After four years of such duty the souls of the warriors and the women could inhabit the Land of Clouds. They would be transformed into birds of fine plumage and sweet song, and they would be able to fly happily and freely among the flowers and suck their honey. After death the souls of the aristocracy inhabited birds or higher animals; but plebeian souls entered into beetles, leeches, and other insects. One tribe, the Mextecs, believed that a cave in their area, high in the mountains, was a gate to Paradise. In it they buried their dead so that souls could the more easily make their way to the happy land.

There was thus a variety of possible fates for the human soul; one's behaviour in life would determine one's future after death and also the way in which one might or might not return to mortal life.

The Mexicans believed that soldiers killed in war, or women who died in childbirth such as the one represented in this Totonac clay figure from Veracruz, went to the House of the Sun, where they remained in perfect content.

THE CALENDAR

It is well known that the Mayas and Aztecs had a highly developed calendar system. In their astronomical calculations, myth and science meet. To understand fully the meaning and position of the various gods in the cosmic plan, we must diverge slightly from the main mythological theme in order to study the calendar.

The Mayas, and probably the Nahua-speaking peoples also, regarded days as animate beings, in fact as gods. Time was thus personified and in no way abstract. Every division of time – the day, the month, the year and so on – was a definite object or entity, and it had to be carried by divine messengers which were represented by numbers. If Plato's god was a mathematician, so too was the Maya-Nahua god-above-all. Numbers were his army, protecting his eternal and infinite domain. An important Maya scholar, J. Eric S. Thompson, explains the Maya view by an analogy with our calendar. If we were to take the date 31 December 1965 as an illustration, then there would be six messengers or bearers. The god of number 31 would carry December on his back. The god of number 1 would be carrying the millennium, the god of number 9 the centuries, the god of number 6 the decades, and the god of number 5 the years. At the end of the year there would be a pause, and the procession would

A Zapotec funerary urn, modelled in clay, from Oaxaca. The figure is the butterfly god, the symbol of rebirth.

reshape itself and start again with the first messenger (1), carrying January, and with the god of number 6 replacing number 5 for the year. In hieroglyphs the messengers were represented carrying their burdens, the weight taken by a strap across the forehead as one can still today see miners raising their loads of ore up the shaft ladders, or peasants carrying wood, charcoal and other wares, trotting with them for incredibly long journeys without tiring. In the hieroglyphs there are also night gods who take over when each day is done.

By the peculiar nature of the calendar, only four gods could start off the load of the new year. Two – Kan, the maize god, and Muluc, rain, would bring good fortune; and two others (Ix and Cauac) were harbingers of disaster.

The cyclical view that the Mayas held of time meant that they saw history in terms of repetition; but the repetition was extended over very long periods for there are inscriptions extant recording a regression of four hundred million years into the past, and others which look at least four thousand years into the future.

Both Mayas and Aztecs based their calendars on cycles of eighteen-day periods arranged in multiples of twenty. Thus 20×18 made 360 days. To these were added five days 'outside the calendar' to form a year, in Maya terminology a *Haab*. In both Nahua and Maya lands people were careful not to fall asleep during the daylight hours of these extra-calendar days, nor to quarrel, nor to trip as they walked. They believed that what they did then they would do forever. People tended to confine themselves to their houses, and were careful not to perform any chores or unpleasant activities, lest they should be committed to these forever.

The 365-day year was corrected in such a way that the Mayas fixed the true passage of the earth about the Sun at 365.2420 days, which is only two ten-thousandths of a day short of modern calculations (365.2422). Our Gregorian calendar fixes the year at 365.2425 days, or three ten-thousandths of a day too long.

A *tun* was a 360-day period. A *katun* was 20×260 days, or 7,200 days, roughly 20 years and exactly 12.5 cycles of Venus. A *baktun* was 20 *katunes*, or 144,000 days, about 400 years. A *pictun* was 20 *baktunes*, or 2,880,000 days, about 8,000 years. A *calabtun* was 20 *pictunes*, or 57,600,000 days, about 158,000 years. A *kinchiltun* was 20 *calabtunes*, or 1,520,000,000 days, about 3 million years. Twenty *kinchiltunes* formed one *alautun*, or 23,040,000,000 days, over 60 million years.

It so happened that a *katun* could end only on a day called *Ahau*, and every 260 *tuns* the same *Ahau*, numbered in a series, would turn up. Within the greater stretches, history would begin to repeat itself at least to the extent of coming once again under the same cosmic influences. For example, *katun 8 Ahau* was believed always to bring disturbances, wars, and political upheavals. In fact an usurping family called Itzá that had ruled over a part of the Maya lands for centuries was not defeated until 1697 A. D., just before the start of a *katun* that spelled tragedy; though whether this coincidence was due to destiny or to an acute suggestibility in the mind of the ruling Itzá, it would be hard to say. The name Itzá means in Mexican a yoke, and the burden of this usurping rule was supposed to have lain upon the Mayas from about the tenth to the sixteenth centuries though there is evidence that some Itzá kings were wise men. One of their greatest prophets predicted that the white man would come. Another high chief, Ta-Itzá, was destined to cause suffering to his beloved princess, Sac-Nicté, who had been betrothed to another prince, Ulmil Itzahal. Ta-Itzá stole Sac-Nicté and presented her to his people in Petén, but the

Xochipilli, the young god of flowers and beauty, love and happiness. One of the thirteen who presided over the hours of the day. Aztec carving from Tlalmanalco.

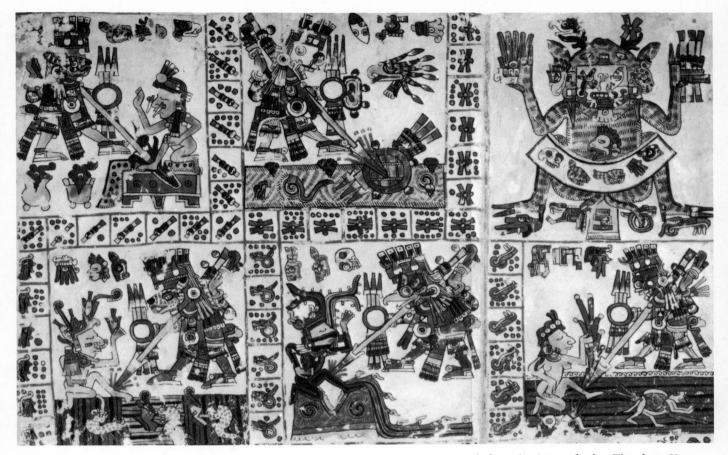

unhappy princess drowned herself in a lake.

Beautiful ceremonies performed by the Itzá are described in one of the *Chilam Balam*:

'Now the wizards vie with one another in taking the shapes of the blue heron and of the humming bird. Then flowers descend from the source of all and from the folds of the Great Hand – nine flowers. When the hearts of the flowers appear, the priests place four branches of flowers on the burning altar of the Sun.'

Probably, then, the dynasty of the Itzá was not consistently bad but merely described the whole cyclical round of cosmic fate. It is difficult to believe that the Yucatán temple site Chichén Itzá, called after these kings, was the product of anything but a high culture.

Within the larger cycle of good and bad fate, and within the cycle of the earth about the Sun, a smaller kind of 'year' was made up of a succession of 260 days, divided into twenty groups of thirteen. This is called in Maya terminology the Tzolkin or 'count of days', and in Aztec the *Tonalpohualli*. In both systems the days always had an accompanying number, so that in the Maya calendar, for instance, the days would run 1 *Ik*, 2 *Akbal*, 3 *Kan* and so forth. But in order to describe a given date exactly one would have to add to this designation its position in the 365-day year. Thus in the old calendars there were various 'sliding scales' or inter-meshed counts allowing very exact descriptions of earthly time in relation to the heavenly bodies.

Both Mayas and Aztecs also subdivided time into periods of fifty-two days. For example the *Tonalpohualli* of the Aztecs was divided into five parts, corresponding to the four compass points and the centre, and having an exact parallel in the 52-year cycle at the end of which the sun had to be revived or creation would end. We should note here that the number 5 was specifically associated with Quetzalcoatl and his quincunx symbol,

Details from the Aztec calendar. The planet Venus, Quetzalcoatl, is manifest here as the Morning Star. The two upper sections show (*left*) that on these days Venus is a danger to Princes and (*right*) the days when Venus destroys warriors. The lower section shows the days when (*left*) crops are in danger; when all things to do with mountains are threatened (*centre*) and the days when Venus is inimical to women and the creatures of the great waters (*right*). The figure in the top right-hand corner is Camaxtli, a god of fate, with the twenty day signs attached to parts of his body. *Codex Borgia*.

and also with Venus, one aspect of Quetzalcoatl. The synodic revolution of Venus (Quetzalcoatl) is 584 days, and these revolutions were grouped by the Nahuas in fives, so that 5 × 584 equalled 2,920 days, or exactly eight years. At the moment when the solar year and the Venus cycle coincided, feasts and rites were dedicated to Xiuhtecuhtli-Huehueteotl, god of the year, god of the centre, standing at the very hub of the cardinal points, just as the *tlecuil*, or brazier, is the hearth at the centre of all indigenous temples and homes. Therefore the god was often associated with that other form of quincunx, the cross, with emphasis on the connections between each point and the centre. The great incense burners with which the priests paid ritual homage to the gods were often shaped as a cross.

We have, then, multiples of 13 × 20 and of 18 × 20 days, of 52 days and of 52 years, and of synodic revolutions of Venus and the planet's conjunction with the calendar year on earth. There was also a division of 73 days which, multiplied by the 260-day cycle, created the 52 years, bring the meshed cycles even closer. And there were lesser 9-day cycles known as Companions of the Night, although some – including the German nineteenth-century investigator, Eduard Seler – think that this was not a cycle of days but of hours, one deity presiding over each hour of darkness.

The nine companions were the fire god Xiuhtecuhtli; Itztli, god of the sacrificial knife; Piltzintecuhtli, a sun god; Cinteotl, the god of maize; Mictlantecuhtli, god of death; Chalchihuitlicue, the water goddess; an earth goddess and goddess of love, Tlazolteutl; Tepeyollotl, the heart of the mountain; and Tlaloc, the rain god.

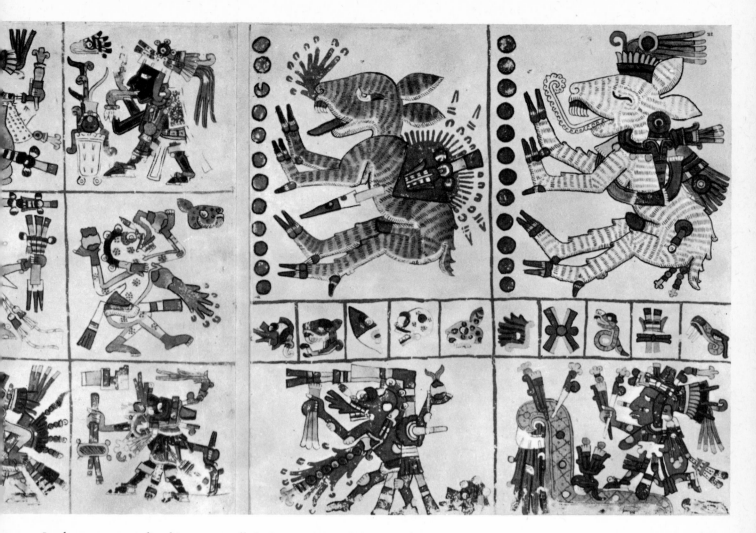

In the same way the thirteen so-called Companions of the Day (some of them duplicated from the night) presided over the hours of daylight; Xiuhtecuhtli; Tlaltecuhtli, an earth god; Chalchihuitlicue; Tonatiuh, the sun god; Tlacolteutl; Mictlantecuhtli; Xochipilli-Cinteotl; Tlaloc; Quetzalcoatl; Tezcatlipoca; Chalmecatecuhtli, god of sacrifice; Tlahuixcalpantecuhtli, god of dawn; and Citlalinicue, goddess of the Milky Way.

The total number of companions adds up to twenty-two hours, so that each ancient Mexican hour must have been longer than that marked by our clocks. Eduard Seler gives us the order of gods for the hours of day and night, with alternative lists from the Mexican investigators given in brackets, in the diagram on page 48.

These Companions of Day and Night are not to be confused with the patron deities of the days, which we shall come to later.

At the end of the 52-day cycles an extra, intercalary period, sometimes of twelve and sometimes of thirteen days, brought the calendar into line with the position of the sun among the stars. The multiple of 13 × 20 days made 260 days; and the cycle of 20-day signs was repeated thirteen times in such a way that only in every 260 days did any given day sign occupy the same place in the 13-day 'week'. The full description of a day could never be merely *cipactli*, *coatl*, or *calli*; a number from one to thirteen had to precede it. A day would therefore be known as One-water-serpent, Two-snake, and so on. No wonder that the priests had their time almost fully occupied with the various calendar-astronomical calculations, and no wonder that numbers such as 7, 9, 13, 20, and 52 were held sacred by the pre-Hispanic peoples.

The twenty Aztec day signs in three leaves from the *Codex Borgia*. The god of each day appears in a separate square, with the accompanying sign in the corner. The first two appear on the bottom of the right-hand leaf. The sequence reads from right to left, continuing on the centre leaf and the leaf on the left, where it follows on the line above, reading from left to the square on the far right of the centre leaf. This continues in the square above and concludes, reading right to left, in the top left square of the left-hand leaf. The first square shows *cipactli*, crocodile, and the last shows *xochitl*, flower.

A clay head of Xipe Totec, an aspect of the shabby and despised god Nanautzin who sacrificed himself in the fire to enable the sun to continue lighting the world. He is also the flayed god and is said to make the seeds germinate in the earth. The skin covering the face is his distinctive representation. Toltec, ninth to thirteenth centuries A.D.

The order of gods for the hours of day and night, according to Eduard Seler.

	NOON	
	Xochipilli-Cinteotl	
	7	
Teoyaomiqui 6		8 Tlaloc
(or preferably Mictlantecutli)		9 Quetzalcoatl
		10 Tezcatlipoca
Tlacolteutl 5		11 Mictlantecutli
Tonatiuh 4		(or Chalmecatecutli)
Chalchihuitlicue 3		12 Tlauizcalpantecutli
Tlaltecutli 2		13 Ilamatecutli
Xiuhtecutli 1		(Citlalinicue according to Mexican investigators)
Tlaloc IX		I Xiuhtecutli
Tepeyollotl VIII		II Itztli
Tlacolteutl VII		III Piltzintecutli–Tonatiuh
Chalchihuitlicue VI		IV Cinteotl
	V	
	Mictlantecutli	
	MIDNIGHT	

From a modern astronomical standpoint the sliding scale was a surprisingly efficient one. For instance, the agricultural-solar calendar of 365 days, multiplied by two 52-year periods, gives 37,960 days; 146 times the 260-day period also gives 37,960 days; and the synodic revolutions of Venus are 584×65, or 37,960 days. So that every 104 years these three sliding scales coincided. Again, five periods of 260 days make 1,300 days, or 44 revolutions of the moon about the earth. Mercury's cycle is 116 days, or about 9×13. The 584-day Venus cycle is 2.25×260. One cycle of Mars is 780 days, or exactly 3×260. Jupiter's cycle is 399 days, roughly 22×18. Saturn's cycle is 378 days, or 360 plus 18. By the sliding scale, the cycles of the planets could be calculated with a degree of accuracy that was remarkable.

The footsteps of the god

Before we study the Maya procession of days, which once again is a symbol of birth, death, and resurrection, we should note the detailed account of creation as given in the *Book of the Month* of the *Chilam Balam*:

'When in days gone by the world had not yet awakened, the Month was born and began to walk alone. Then said his maternal grandmother, then said his aunt, and his paternal grandmother, and his sister-in-law: "Why was it said that we should see men on the road?" Thus they wondered as they walked, for there were no men in those days. And then they reached the East, and they said, "Somebody has passed this way. Here are his footprints."

'"Measure it with your foot," said the World Mother, or so they tell.

'Then he measured the footprints of God, the Word. That is why it was called "counting off the world by footprints"... When the Month had been born, he created what is known as a day, and he created heaven and earth in the form of a ladder: water, earth, rocks, trees. He created all things on earth and in the sea. In *One Chuen* he brought forth from himself divinity and created heaven and earth. In *Two Eb* he created the first ladder so that God could descend into the midst of the sky and the sea. Neither land nor stones nor trees existed then. In *Three Ben* he made all things, the whole diversity of creation; things in heaven and in the sea and on the earth. In *Four Ix* heaven and earth embraced each other. In *Five Men* things moved into action. In *Six Cib* the first candle was made, and thus it was that light was created where there had been neither sun nor moon. In *Seven C'haban* the earth was born where there had been none in days gone by. In *Eight Edznab* he rooted hands and feet upon earth. In *Nine Cauac* for the first time there was an attempt to create hell. In *Ten Ahau* bad men went to hell because God the Word had not yet appeared. In *Eleven Imix* stones and trees were made. In *Twelve Ik* wind was created. And that is the reason why he is called *Ik* (Spirit), because in him there is no death. In *Thirteen Akbal* he took water and moistened clay and shaped the body of a man.

'In *One Kan* his spirit was afflicted because of the evil he had created. In *Two Chicchan* evil made its appearance and could be seen by men. In *Three Cimi* death was invented. It came about that God our Father invented the first death.'

At this point in the *Chilam Balam* manuscript there is a blank space corresponding to *Four Man-ik*, the day in which the Spirit passes over.

'In *Five Lamat* he invented the great reservoir of the great sea lake. In *Six Muluc* all the valleys were filled with earth before the world had awakened. And it came to pass that a false voice of God our Father entered into them all, when there was neither voice in heaven nor stones nor trees, in days gone by. And then, one after another, the days were put to the test, and they said: "Thirteen... plus seven form a cluster (of twenty)..." Thus was the month created when earth awakened, and when heaven and earth and the trees and stones were made. All was created by God our Father and by his Word. His divinity appeared where there was neither heaven nor earth, and by its power he became a cloud, and created the Universe. And his great power and majesty shook the heavens.'

These twenty days, the footprints of the god, turn out to be nothing less than the symbolic representation of man's spiritual pilgrimage. They are twenty steps up and down the ladder, beginning with *Imix*, from *Im*, the womb. The first day starts the child off on his journey through life. On the second, *Ik*, spirit or breath is bestowed upon him when he is still within the womb. On the third, *Akbal*, he is born of water (the ancient pre-Hispanic peoples had baptismal ceremonies). On the fourth, *Kan*, he begins to know evil; and on the fifth, *Chicchan*, he gathers together all the experience of his life. On the sixth, *Cimi*, he dies. On the seventh *Man-Ik*, from *Manzal-Ik* (pass through the spirit) he overcomes death.

Now he must plunge into the lower regions; he must struggle to overcome the material state. This is the eighth day, *Lamat*, the sign of Venus. On the ninth day, *Muluc*, he reaps the reward of his effort; and on the tenth, *Oc*, he enters fully into the uttermost depths of matter in order, on the eleventh day, *Chuen*, to burn without flame. In other words, he suffers

Onyx marble bowl, late classic Maya style. On the side shown *top* a priest is presenting a votive jar bearing the *kan* cross. *Bottom*, another aspect of the bowl, the decoration of which records an offering, probably to the North Star god, on a particular day, Imix. The symbols represent the Earth. The inscription on the rim refers to both the god and the day, and to a 'distance number' reading to and from the day 4 Ahau when all twenty-year periods – *Katuns* – ended.

Overleaf, left: the Temple of the Inscriptions at Palenque, one of the great Maya cities. The temple was built about the sixth century A.D. and a crypt was used as a mausoleum for nobles and priests. Right: the temple at Malinalco. The building was begun about 1475 and remained unfinished when the Aztec nation fell to the Spaniards under Cortés. The temple contains a circular shrine of the knightly orders of eagle and jaguar.

the greatest possible agony. On the twelfth day, *Eb*, he begins to climb the ladder, a long process which continues through the thirteenth day, *Ben*, (which represents growing maize) until on the fourteenth *Ix* (the jaguar god), he is washed entirely clean. This allows him on the fifteenth day, *Men*, to become perfect, but still he does not possess the full light of consciousness, which comes to him on the sixteenth day, *Cib*. On the seventeenth day, *C'haban*, he shakes off the last traces of ash clinging to him from the material world. 'Ash' is the word specifically used and it suggests that he has been purged by fire. On the eighteenth day, *Edznab*, he is made perfect. By the nineteenth day, *Cauac*, his divine nature is manifest. On the twentieth and last day, *Ahau* (god), he becomes one with the divinity.

There could scarcely be a clearer picture of physical birth, followed by death to the world of forms, and a rebirth on the plane of pure spirit. A distinction between the two processes of universal creation on the one hand and the cycle of man's birth and death on the other is clearly made. In the *Chilam Balam* description of the whole of creation, the series of days begins with *Chuen* (burning without flame), whereas the human cycle begins with the womb. The idea of creation beginning with a burning without flame exists in the Nahua myth of creation, where the universe comes into being through the voluntary suffering of the humblest of the gods. The creation of the days, according to the *Chilam Balam* ends with *Muluc* (and by inference with *Oc*, which for some reason is not mentioned in the *Chilam Balam* version). This is the point where the pilgrim enters fully into matter.

The Aztec-Nahua day-names give a more confused picture, but if we begin from the first day of the series, and not from the eleventh as in the Maya journey through twenty steps, we get interesting parallels on some rungs of the ladder. The Aztec days, their compass points, and their patron deities, are as follows:

1.	Cipactli. Water-serpent	E	Tonacatecuhtli. Male creator
2.	Ehecatl. Wind god	N	Quetzalcoatl. As wind god
3.	Calli. Temple	W	Tepeyollotl. Heart of the mountain
4.	Quetzpallin. Lizard	S	Huehuecoyotl. God of dance
5.	Coatl. Snake	E	Chalchihuitlicue. Water goddess
6.	Miquiztli. Death	N	Tecciztecatl. The moon god, he who is to be found in the innermost twist of the conch shell
7.	Mazatl. Deer	W	Tlaloc
8.	Tochtli. Rabbit	S	Mayahuel. Goddess of drink
9.	Atl. Water	E	Xiuhtecuhtli. Fire god
10.	Itzcuintli. Dog	N	Mictlantecuhtli. God of death
11.	Ozmatli. Monkey	W	Xochipilli. God of flowers
12.	Malinalli. Grass or thorns used in penitential acts	S	Patecatl. Husband of Mayahuel
13.	Acatl. Reed used for arrow shafts	E	Tezcatlipoca
1.	Ocelotl. The Mexican tiger	N	Tlacolteutl. Earth goddess
2.	Quauhtli. Eagle	W	Xipe. The flayed god
3.	Cozcaquauhtli. Vulture	S	Itzpapalotl. Obsidian butterfly
4.	Ollin. Movement	E	Xolotl. Twin to Quetzalcoatl
5.	Tecpatl. Stone knife	N	Tezcatlipoca
6.	Quiahuitl. Rain	W	Chantico. Fire goddess
7.	Xochitl. Flower	S	Xochiquetzal. Flower goddess

Huehueteotl or Xiutecuhtli, the fire god, one of the Companions of the Night. His worship was the occasion for a cruel sacrifice, when human victims were caste alive on burning coals before their hearts were removed. This head is part of a jadeite statue found at Teotihuacán.

The male creator stands with the water serpent at the head of the list. Then wind is breathed into the still formless mass, and a temple is created with wisdom (Tepeyollotl, the heart of the mountain) at its core. After two more days we reach death and the god folded in the shell, ready in the womb to be reborn of water. It is interesting that twice (at the signs Atl and Quiauitl) the day sign and the ruling deity make a firewater pair, representing 'burning water', one of the paradoxes which according to Nahua philosophy had to be solved by enlightenment. Similarly the deity representing 'blossoming war' (the obsidian butterfly, the war within the heart that leads to truth) stands opposite the predatory vulture.

As to the compass points, the years beginning with eastern signs were supposed to be fertile; those beginning with the north, variable; those with the west, good for man but bad for vegetation; and those with the south, hot and waterless. The Companions of Day and Night, and also the patrons of each of the twenty days, spread a special influence, either good, bad, or indifferent, and the science of Mexican and Maya astrology was based on the interpretation of the various combinations of signs. If a child was born on a good sign he was baptised at once; if on a bad, the evil influence might be mitigated by holding his baptism later to coincide with a good omen. The twenty day-signs may have been related each to a given heavenly body, but the chronicles shed little light on this aspect of the calendar. In the Maya series, the order of creation of the days emphasises the essential suffering inherent in matter, and the fact that the spirit must of necessity live within the material world; while the calendar order of the days stresses the corollary, that a man is only fully born and fully alive when he has overcome matter and reached pure spirit. Thus an equilibrium is established between man's inner and outer worlds. Matter must not be denied, but if man lives only in matter, his purpose on earth is not fulfilled. Evidently the Mayas did not make the mistake of submerging themselves in inner light while forgetting the outer world, though it is very possible that the degeneration of both Maya and Nahua religions, which had occurred before the Spaniards arrived in the New World, was brought about because the earlier equilibrium maintained between the two aspects of creation – matter and spirit – was lost.

A priest's head carved in relief in slatestone. The disk formed the back of a mirror which had a reflecting surface of iron pyrites. Totonac style, from the Veracruz region.

Below: a jaguar from one of the carved friezes at Teotihuacán. In ancient Mexico the jaguar was the creature of the era of the Fourth Sun – the era which preceded ours.

Right: an Aztec funerary mask with jade inclusion in the mosaics. The peoples of ancient Mexico were masters of the art of mask carving and decorating, using them to represent their gods, as votive offerings, as cult objects or, as in this case, to accompany the burial of persons of high rank.

Quetzalcoatl, the morning star or the planet Venus, being swallowed by the serpent, earth, as day breaks and the sun returns. From the *Codex Vaticanus*.

THE LEGEND OF THE FIVE SUNS

It may well be that the era of the Fifth Sun, in which we are now supposed to be living, is in decline. Creatures on earth suffer continual testing by the gods, and if any species fails it perishes with the Sun to which it belongs. Both Maya and Nahua myths affirm this, and there are various versions of the legend of the birth and death of Suns.

In a manuscript called the *Annals of Cuauhtitlán*, one Nahua version relates that the first of five eras – four of which have long since died – was symbolised by an ocelot. This was the reign of instinctive power dwelling in animal form and in the dark. None of its human inhabitants were saved from extinction – the ocelots devoured them all. Then came the Sun of Air, the era of pure spirit that might at some future date become incarnate. But for the moment the necessary redeeming principle was absent, and the men of this age were turned into monkeys. After this came the Sun of the Rain of Fire, but its creatures were destined also to perish, except for the birds who were able to fly to safety. Last of the four Suns was the Sun of Water, during which the fishes of the sea were created. But this Sun perished by flood.

The Four Suns of animal energy earth, air, fire, and water evidently represent the four elements. Each by itself was doomed to die. Only when the Fifth Sun was born – *Naollin* (Four Movements) – was it possible for the separate elements in creation to come together and form the living sun of today. We cannot, however, take it for granted that this Sun is immortal. It can become immortal only if mankind climbs the ladder of redemption which we have seen represented in the names of the twenty days of the Maya calendar. The Nahuas too had a symbolism for this regenerative process that is the chief aim of creation: if the aim is not fulfilled, the world must be destroyed.

A folk dance performed today by groups of Mexican Indians, and which is evidently a vestige of preconquest ritual, represents the Four Suns dancing and dying each in turn. They come to life again only through the power of the Fifth Sun, who gyrates at great speed in the centre. Again we see the four elements inert and helpless when separate, life-giving when joined in movement.

In some versions of the Nahua legend the order of creation is changed. First comes the Sun of Water, then of Air, then of Fire, and then of Earth. One story tells how, when the first Sun was destroyed, a human couple sheltered in a cave and were thus saved from the flood. A man and a woman were also able to escape from the second cataclysm, and they took with them the Promethean gift of fire which was in its turn to destroy the Third Sun. When the Fourth Sun came to an end, man rescued certain nourishing plants and flowers and was able to begin life anew in the era of the Fifth and present Sun.

During one of these ages, the supreme god sent for the human pair, Tata and Nena, and told them to make a hole in a great tree and to hide in it. When the flood came they would be saved, they were told, but only if they were not greedy and did not eat more than a single maize cob each. The man and woman remained safely in their hole until the waters receded. When at last they emerged, they saw a fish, and they made a fire on which to roast it. The gods saw the smoke rise into the air and were very angry. As a punishment Tata and Nena were amputated of a portion of their heads and transformed into dogs. Because they had disobeyed the gods, they forfeited that part of the brain which distinguishes man from animals.

THE TWINS OF THE POPOL VUH

The sanctuary of the Temple of the Jaguars at Chichén Itzá, on the wall of the ball court. The adventures of the twins of the *Popol Vuh* are reflected in much of Mayan art and architecture: they escaped death in a House of Jaguars and defeated their enemies on a ball court.

The gods of ancient America were perpetually trying to evolve a living thing that would have the capacity of knowing and worshipping its maker. They found this no easy task, and the Maya *Popol Vuh* is in essence the story of their efforts. The deer and the birds and all four-footed animals could only hiss and scream, says the sacred book, but could shape no word of praise. Above all, they could not pronounce their maker's name. Firmly they had to be told: 'We shall fashion other creatures to obey us. Accept your lot. Your flesh shall be torn apart. Thus shall it be...'

And a little later the chorus of gods cries out in a fit almost of pessimism: 'What shall we do to be invoked and remembered on earth? We have made attempts already with our first creatures, our first creations, but we could not persuade them to praise or adore us. We must try to make obedient creatures who will feed and sustain us.'

So they made a man of clay, but he was too soft and had no mind. He could not stand upright, and he dissolved too easily in water. Then they made men of wood, and these could talk and multiply but had neither souls nor minds. They forgot their Creator and walked on all fours. A flood was sent to destroy them, and even the implements they invented

56

rose against them – the earthen pots, the plates and skillets and the grinding stones – and accused them of hard-heartedness. These inanimate things had been left to blacken on the fire as if they could feel no pain. The dogs who were the wooden men's domestic animals also accused them, and in the commotion that followed the men were turned into monkeys, simulating man but without intelligence.

Next there arose an extraordinary impostor called Vucub-Caquix, who professed to be the sun, the light and the moon: 'My eyes are silver, bright and shining like precious stones, like emeralds. My teeth shine like perfect stones, like the face of heaven. My nose shines from afar like the moon. My throne is of silver, and the face of the earth is alight when I stand before my throne.'

It was obvious to the gods that before true men could be made, this impostor had to be overthrown, and a large part of the *Popol Vuh* is concerned with the war waged against him by the heavenly twins Hunapú god of the hunt, and Ixbalanqué, whose name means 'little jaguar'.

The twins noticed that Vucub-Caquix liked the fruit of a certain tree, so they lay in ambush, and when he came for his daily meal they fired arrows and wounded him. In the ensuing struggle the evil giant was able to unhinge one of Hunapú's arms and to make off with it. In the task of retrieving the arm the twins enlisted the help of an old man and an old woman. These two went in search of Vucub-Caquix and found him suffering from toothache as a result of one of his wounds. Claiming that they could cure his pain, and knowing that his strength lay in his teeth, the old people extracted them and replaced them with grains of maize. They also offered to cure his eyes, which they gouged out so that by now his vaunted beauty had all been taken from him and he was shown up as a hollow-cheeked old creature. The old couple did not fail, while attending the giant, to retrieve Hunapú's arm, which was easily fixed back into position.

This was not by any means the end of the twins' struggle against evil, however, for Vucub-Caquix had two sons who took up the battle on their father's behalf. The elder was Zipacná, 'creator of mountains'. Four hundred warriors were fetching a log to prop up the roof of their house when Zipacná offered to help. He proved strong enough to carry the wood all by himself. The four hundred, who were on the side of the heavenly twins, then lured Zipacná into a deep pit where they hoped to bury him. The giant, seeing the trap, burrowed out an exit from which he was able to escape, leaving the four hundred rejoicing in their supposed victory. Gloating, they waited for the ants to come and devour their victim's corpse; and sure enough they were soon able to observe armies of them carrying bits of hair and finger-nail which Zipacná had cut off to lull the enemy into a sense of false security. Overcome with delight at the apparent success of their plot, the four hundred began a drunken orgy which put them at the mercy of Zipacná, who was still very much alive and only waiting for an opportunity to pull the house down about the heads of the four hundred. Not one of them escaped this disaster, but long after their death they were transformed into stars.

During the day Zipacná used to hunt along the river for fish and crabs, and during the night he carried mountains on his back. Hunapú and Ixbalanqué, wishing to avenge the four hundred, made a model, a delicious-looking and large crab. They put this in a cave at the foot of a high mountain, and then lured Zipacná inside. He was about to eat the apparently succulent crab when the mountain fell on top of him and crushed him.

However the second son of Vucub-Caquix, a demolisher of mountains,

A mask of the bat god. In the *Popol Vuh* he is Camozotz, who destroyed the twins' father by tearing off his head. Jadeite, from Monte Albán. The eyes and teeth are made of shell.

A painted clay figure from Colima showing a dog carrying an ear of maize.

still remained at large. The heavenly twins went in search of him and engaged him in friendly conversation as he was levelling out a mountain. When he asked their names they said they had none but were merely hunters with gun and trap. They offered to lead this second son, Cabraca, to a splendid mountain. On their march he was surprised to find that they did not need ammunition in their blowpipes but could bring down birds with no more than a puff of air. The boys roasted the birds golden brown and Cabraca could not resist this tempting meal. He did not know that the twins had basted the birds with poisonous earth; and so the second son of Vucub-Caquix met his end.

It so happened that the father of the twins, one Hun-Hunapú, had been lured to the underworld to play ball. There he had been defeated and killed, his head hung on a calabash tree as a warning to any who dared interfere with the underworld people called Xibalba. But the calabash tree, which had been barren, immediately bore fruit and was venerated as being miraculous. A maiden heard the story and went in wonder to gaze upon it. Hun-Hunapú's skull spoke to her from its branches, asking her what she wished. 'All the other fruits are only skulls,' he told her, 'and will do you no good.' But the maiden insisted and stretched her hand out toward the skull, which spat into her palm and said: 'In my saliva and spittle I have given you my descendants. Now my head is uncovered. It is only a fleshless skull. Even so are the heads of great princes. It is only the flesh that makes them seem handsome, but when they die men fear their bones. So also is the nature of our progeny, which are like saliva and spittle... They do not lose their substance when they go, but they bequeath it to others. The image of the lord, of the sage, of the orator does not vanish but he leaves it to the sons and daughters whom he procreates. Even so have I done unto you. Return to earth and believe my words for it shall be so.'

The maiden, made pregnant by the spittle, gave birth to Hunapú and

The sacred city of Chichén Itzá dates from the
sixth century A.D., and was the largest of the
Toltec–Maya centres. The pyramid, seen here from
the platform of the Temple of the Warriors,
was dedicated to the plumed serpent.

A palmate stone from Veracruz representing a sacrificed man – the incision can be seen which allowed for the removal of the heart. The *palmas* were part of the remarkably heavy accoutrements of the ball game players. Classic Veracruz style.

Ixbalanqué. But these two were at once persecuted by their envious half-brothers who had been models of good behaviour until then but who now idled and played the flute and sang while the twins had to provide them with food. To teach them a lesson, Hunapú and Ixbalanqué changed the jealous brothers into monkeys, and even their doting grandmother could not help laughing at their appearance.

Hunapú and Ixbalanqué believed it was their mission to go down to the underworld to avenge their father's death. In the nether regions they were subjected to a series of trials. At first they were made to enter a place called the House of Gloom and were given pine torches and cigars to provide them with comfort. They resisted the temptation of lighting either, and the next day were able to defeat the Xibalba in a ball game. Nevertheless the Xibalba had still the upper hand. The twins were shut up in a second prison, the House of Knives. Not only did they pass the night unharmed, but next day they were able to enlist the help of the knives and also of ants in order to cut a bouquet of flowers to present to their captors.

Next the twins passed the night in the House of Cold, but they found old logs and made a fire and did not die. Another trial was in the House of Jaguars, but the boys threw bones to the beasts and themselves escaped harm. They passed unscathed through the House of Fire, but nearly met total defeat in the House of Bats where Hunapú's head was struck off. The Xibalba took it to the ball court and hung it up as a trophy.

There now occurred an incident which seems to be connected with the idea of finding a suitable food for man. Ixbalanqué called all the animals together and asked them to choose the food of their liking. Some selected putrid stuff, others grass, others stone, others earth. But the turtle, as he waddled along behind the rest, climbed onto Hunapú's shoulders and took the shape of his head. It was no easy matter to model in Hunapú's features, but at length this was done.

Once more in possession of his full faculties, Hunapú joined his brother in planning the defeat of the Xibalba on the ball court. They caused the ball to bounce far over the court where a rabbit had been stationed in order to chase it and to encourage the underworld people to run after him. This he effectively did, allowing time for Ixbalanqué to steal back Hunapú's real head. When the Xibalba team returned, they found their opponents much stronger and the game ended in a tie.

By now the Xibalba were desperate to end the contest, and decided upon the drastic measure of burning the twins. They prepared a bonfire and then suggested that they should all fly four times over the flames. However, there was no need for such a ruse because Hunapú and Ixbalanqué, knowing by then their prowess had won them immortality, were fully prepared for death and threw themselves willingly onto the flames. Five days later they rose from the dead and appeared in the guise of fishermen, ragged and unkempt but gay enough to put on a dancing show for an assembled company and to work miracles. They burned houses and caused them to reappear undamaged, and cut themselves to bits but returned to life. The lords of the Xibalba were amazed and asked for a repeat performance. The twins feigned reluctance, professing to be ashamed of their ragtaggle appearance, but at length they were persuaded. Having sacrificed themselves and returned to life, they did the same for the Xibalba rulers except that the process of reversal was omitted. When the underworld plebeians saw that their rulers were dead, they admitted defeat and begged for mercy: 'Thus were the lords of the underworld overcome. Only by a miracle and only by transforming themselves could they have achieved their purpose.' They made themselves known to the underworld survivors, for the first time giving their names, and they pronounced sentence on their enemies: 'Because your great power and your race no longer exist, and because you deserve no mercy, you shall be brought low and shall no longer be allowed to play ball. You shall occupy yourselves fashioning earthen pots and tubs and grinding-stones for maize. Only the sons of the undergrowth and the desert shall be allowed to speak to you. The sons of nobles and the civilised vassals shall have no truck with you and shall shun you. Sinners, the wicked and sad, the unfortunate and the vicious, these shall welcome you...'

As to the twins, their grandmother was so delighted with their achievements that she worshipped them and gave them the title 'Those at the Centre'; green grasses grew in the house where they lived. Having avenged their father's death they became centred in themselves, and they were later translated to heaven where one became the Sun and the other the Moon. Their redeeming power was such that the four hundred killed by Zipacná also rose to heaven and became the stars – companions to the twins in the sky.

After this arduous preliminary work, after the descent of the twins to the underworld, their trials and triumph and translation, it became possible once more to return to the task of creating man 'to nourish and sustain' the gods. Four animals gathered together the special food, maize. These were the cat or jaguar, the coyote, the parrot, and the crow: 'Thus they discovered food, and this it was that entered into the flesh of man incarnate, of man made man. This was his blood. Of this was man's blood made. So maize was discovered because of the labour of man's forebears.'

The 'maize stone' from Veracruz. The god of water and the god of fertility preside over the planting of maize to ensure plenty for mankind. Nahua-Toltec culture, thirteenth to fifteenth centuries A.D.

A head modelled in clay, from the Veracruz region. A fine example of Totonac art.

Right: a worshipper, probably a priest, kneels to make an offering. A parrot seems to form part of his costume but it may also have been an offering. This vivid example of Maya low relief carving is from Jonuta in the state of Tabasco.

The first four created men had no parents but were born miraculously out of the effort of the gods. They were intelligent, far-sighted, and could contemplate all heaven and earth without having to move from a single spot. And they gave thanks to their creators.

But their very excellence was their undoing for the gods feared they might become puffed up with arrogance and self-confidence, and they decided to limit their powers. The great god who was the Heart of Heaven blew mist into men's eyes and clouded their sight so that it was like a looking-glass dimmed by breath. Their last state reflects the situation of man to this day: with intelligence of a kind unpossessed by animals, but seeing creation as through a glass darkly.

The final chapters of the *Popol Vuh* seem to be a straight history of the tribes that issued from the first four men and their wives. The author of the tale was an anonymous Guatemalan Indian who lived after the Spanish conquest and was influenced by Christianity. In a preamble he tells us that his version is only a reconstruction of a narrative written down long before but 'concealed from the searcher and the thinker'.

'Splendid were the descriptions and the tales of how all heaven and all earth were created and divided into four parts; how the whole was split and the sky divided. And the measuring rod was brought and was stretched out over the sky and the earth, to the four angles and corners as was told by the Creator and Maker, the Mother and Father of Life, of all created things, He who gives breath and thought, She who engenders children, He who protects people's happiness and that of the human race, the wise man, he who meditates on the goodness of all that exists in heaven and on earth and in the lakes and sea.'

Splendid as the best passages of the *Popol Vuh* may be, one feels that

something has been omitted from the twins' adventures, which flag and appear juvenile at times. It is easy enough to bring miracles out of a hat when all the laws of creation can be suspended at the stroke of a pen, and one does not feel that Hunapú and Ixbalanqué earned their triumph by self-sacrifice or that they acquired their powers by any hard road, as the plumed serpent Quetzalcoatl did. The original story may well have expressed a greater sense of compassion and of genuine effort at spiritual transformation, however, for the basic and familiar clues are all there: the need for worship; the absolute necessity of finding the right food for man; the inevitable process of a descent to the underworld before regeneration can take place; the overcoming of self-destroying pride and vanity and unmerciful power.

A tale told today in the state of Veracruz is very similar in certain aspects to the *Popol Vuh* story and shows not only that Maya influence spread northward along the coast but also that the legend of the origin of maize was and still is at the core of American Indian thought.

The Vera Cruz maize legend

In the Veracruz version of the story, maize is represented by a clever little fellow called Homshuk. An old couple had discovered him, hatched out of an egg. Even at the moment of his birth his hair was golden, and as soft as the silk down which clings to the ears of maize. After seven days of life his adventures began.

He was jeered at by lesser breeds like minnows and thrushes and other small creatures who declared him ridiculous, not understanding that he was inherently noble and specially endowed. He killed those who made fun of him but his foster-parents became uneasy; they feared the strange child, and decided to murder him while he slept. But they completely misunderstood the child's nature – it was only his mortal shape which lay asleep, his real self was outside, on the roof. The plot recoiled on the head of his foster-father, who was killed instead, and the boy was then persecuted by his foster-mother.

He warned her; 'Let me be. I am very strong and I can destroy you. I am destined to give food to all mankind.'

She paid no heed, and one day tried to destroy him by surrounding him in a curtain of flame. But he managed to escape, and after some wandering made his way to the seashore. There he sat down and began to play on a drum.

The drumming was heard from far away by a great lord, Huracán, who sent a messenger to find out who was making all the noise. To the messenger Homshuk replied;

'I am he who sprouts at the knees. I am he who flowers.'

Huracán thought that the boy was trying to avoid giving his name; he must be an evil spirit, a *nagual*, who wished to remain unknown and thus beyond harm. In the face of what seemed persistent animosity, Homshuk invoked the help of a tortoise who carried him across the sea to the very bastion of Huracán himself.

Here, for offenders against the great lord, there were three kinds of prison. In one there were serpents, in another rapacious tigers, and in another arrows in constant flight. After a night spent in the serpent prison Homshuk was found next morning sitting quietly on the hungry viper's back. The same thing happened with the tigers. The arrows, too, fell harmlessly to the ground and with extreme docility – considering their magical nature – allowed themselves to be made into a bundle for his use in protecting himself, so that he might fulfil the task of providing food for mankind. So the redeemer Homshuk vanquished in turn man's serpentine instincts, his dark tiger nature, and his penetrating, arrow-like, human wickedness. Huracán however was still unable to understand the true nature of his adversary, and invited him to a stone-throwing competition. This Homshuk won with the aid of a woodpecker who, when the lad's stone had been cast, made the characteristic pecking sound which seemed to suggest that the stone was rebounding far away across the ocean. Huracán's stone on the other hand made no sound at all, and Homshuk was conceded the victory.

Then Huracán decreed that Homshuk be swung in a hammock over the ocean, but when Homshuk had reached half way over the water he returned, saying that he could see already how easy the journey was going to be, and that Huracán and his people should go first. After a disastrous voyage Huracán capitulated and offered to keep the lad well watered – it seems as if by now he had taken plant form – so that the maize might grow for man's sustenance.

The details may be different, but the general similarity to the *Popol Vuh* story is clear enough, and we now see that the contest between Huracán, the Heart of Heaven, and the twins (in the *Popol Vuh*) or Homshuk (in the Veracruz story) was a contest not so much between good and evil as between the unharnessed forces of nature (Huracán) and the control exercised by what the Nahua poets would have called a 'man made man', a man who had found the true food, maize, which in so many parts of the world has been a symbol of death and rebirth. The key to an interpretation of the story lies in the fact that Homshuk is hatched out of an egg into a higher life. There is also his pretence at sleep when he was really outside on the roof, surveying the whole scene and in command of it, so that he could kill the incomprehending man, his foster-father, and escape from the old woman. And again there are Homshuk's words to the serpents and the tigers and the arrows: 'I am a strong man, and I must live in order to give food to mankind.' But even more striking is the description he gives of himself, 'I am he who flowers.'

The Veracruz legend forms a link between the *Popol Vuh* and the legends of the Mexican plumed serpent which we shall study later. The struggle between Huracán and the twins, or Huracán and Homshuk, is the same struggle we shall find between the redeeming plumed serpent Quetzalcoatl and the contradictory, wayward Tezcatlipoca. The egg theme and the hatching of a creature with totally new possibilities is echoed in some frescoes found in a priest's dwelling at Teotihuacán near the site of the monumental pyramids.

The Homshuk story is also connected with a theme found in fairy tales the world over, of a very small or very lowly creature whose magical capacities are so great as to give power over giants and other strong adversaries. This theme is common in surviving pre-Hispanic folk lore, as for example in the story of a man who, however many trees he felled during the day, always found them standing on the following morning. A tiny supernatural creature was defeating all his efforts to clear away the timber. There is also the story of a man who mourned his dead wife because he now had nobody to cook for him. To his astonishment, when he returned home one evening he found the floor clean and freshly swept, freshly-prepared maize pancakes and all kinds of food were ready for him. One day, returning home early, the man noticed the skin of his faithful dog lying on the floor and, much to his astonishment, a beautiful woman bending over the cooking pot. Unknown to him, his lowly dog had been his housekeeper.

Left: this Olmec carving from the Veracruz region has a strong resemblance to many Egyptian low reliefs. The bearded figure shown here is probably a priest; the yoke around the waist and the elaborate headdress suggesting a connection with a ball game ritual.

Below: a ball-game marker, carved from stone. From Teotihuacán.

The temple of Tulum, a city founded by the Mayas in the sixth century A.D. near the seashore of Quintana Roo. The holiness of the temple persists – even today it is used by the Indians for religious rites, and they burn the same incense known to the Mayas.

MEN OF GOLD

Returning now to the theme that man, if he is to be truly man, must praise his maker, we find a particularly delightful peasant version of it put by the Mexican novelist Rosario Castellanos into the mouth of her own childhood's nannie. It is probably as near as possible a verbatim account from this illiterate but nevertheless wise and cultured old woman. The story deserves to be quoted in full for its beauty and humanity and because it is evidence that the old myths live still in the minds of the peasants of south-east Mexico and Guatemala – the one-time Maya lands:

'...They were only four in number, the lords in heaven. Each one sat on his chair and rested. For the earth had already been made, just as we see it now, its lap heaped high with bounty. The ocean had already been made, before which everyone who sees it trembles. The wind had already been made to be the guardian over all things. But man was not yet made. Then one of the four lords, the one dressed in yellow, said:

'"We'll make man, so that he may know us and his heart may be consumed with gratitude like a grain of incense."

'The other three agreed with a nod, and went to look for moulds in which to work.

'"What shall we make men of?" they asked.

66

'And the one who was dressed in yellow took a lump of mud and with his fingers drew in the face and the arms and the legs. The other three watched him and gave their consent. But when the little clay man was finished and was put to the test of water, he crumbled away.

'"Let's make a man of wood," said the one dressed in red. The others agreed. So he who was dressed in red lopped off a branch and with the blade of a knife he marked the features in. When the wooden man was made he was put to the test of water and his limbs floated; they didn't fall to pieces, and his features were not rubbed out. The four lords were satisfied. But when the mannikin was put to the test of fire he began to crackle and lose his shape.

'The four lords spent a whole night in parley until one of them, the one who was dressed in black, said, "My advice is that we make a man of gold."

'And he untied the gold he kept knotted in his handkerchief, and between the four of them they modelled him. One pulled out his nose, another stuck in his teeth, another drew the snail-shell of his ears. When the golden man was finished they tested him in water and in fire and the golden man came out even more beautiful and resplendent than before. Then the four lords looked at one another satisfied. And they set the gold man on the ground, and they waited, hoping he would recognize them and give them praise. But the gold man did not move, he did not even blink: he was quite silent. And his heart was like the stone of the sapodilla, very hard and dry. Then three of the four lords asked the one who had not yet given his opinion:

'"What shall we make man of?"

'And this last one, who was dressed neither in yellow nor in red nor in black, for he wore a garment that had no colour at all, said: "Let's make man out of flesh." And with his machete he cut off the fingers of his left hand. And the fingers jumped into the air and fell into the midst of things, and never suffered the tests of water and fire. The four lords could scarcely make out what the men of flesh looked like, because distance had shrunk them to the size of ants. The effort they made to see the men of flesh inflamed the four lords' eyes, and with so much rubbing of them they grew drowsy. The one with the yellow robe yawned, and his yawn opened the mouths of the other three. And they fell asleep, for they were tired and old. In the meantime on earth the men of flesh scurried to and fro like ants. They had already learned which fruit is good to eat, with what big leaves they could protect themselves from the rain, and which animals don't bite.

'One day they were astonished to see standing in front of them the man of gold. His glitter struck them between the eyes, and when they touched him their hands turned cold as if they had touched a snake. They stood there waiting for the man of gold to speak. The time came to eat, and the men of flesh gave the man of gold a morsel. The time came to go away, and the men of flesh carried the man of gold with them. And day by day the hardness of the heart of the man of gold was softened, until the word of gratitude the four lords had placed within him rose to his lips.

'The lords woke up to hear their names pronounced among the psalms of praise. And they looked to see what had happened on earth while they were sleeping. And they approved what they saw. And from that moment they called the man of gold rich and the men of flesh poor. And they ordered things in such a way that the rich man should care for the poor and shelter them, since it was the rich man who benefited by the poor men's acts. And the lords so ordered it that the poor should

The goddess Mayahuel seated on a shell shared by a serpent and a tortoise. Behind her is a maguey plant in flower. As a farmer's wife she discovered that the juice of the plant, when fermented, made a beverage inducing content – pulque. For this benefit to both gods and men she was made a goddess. *Codex Laud.* Bodleian Library.

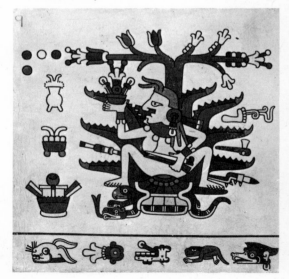

The ancient Mexicans were well-versed in the properties of plants which contained vision-inducing drugs, and regarded them as a boon from the gods. This leaf from the *Codex Magliabecchi*, which dates from the years immediately after the conquest, shows an Indian (bottom right) eating a magic mushroom. Xipe Totec, god of the growing seed, can be seen in the upper left-hand corner and the maize goddess Chicomecoatl in the upper right. The god of death Mictlantecuhtli watches, bottom right.

Below: a ceremonial axe-head, Totonac style, carved in the features of an ocelot. From the Veracruz region.

answer for the rich before the face of Truth. That is why our law says that no rich man can enter heaven if a poor man does not lead him by the hand.'

Communicating with the gods

The stress laid in the myths on the need for communication between men and gods demonstrates the enormous importance that was attached to revelation. Communication of this kind could be achieved if the neophyte purified his heart and mind, so that the gods could speak through men in poetry and song, and so that men might communicate their longing to the gods. Whereas the purification of heart and mind required fasting and presumably mental and emotional disciplines (there are many recorded instructions to the students in the colleges suggesting that discipline was rigorous), the process of getting into touch with the deities could be intensified and quickened by the use of drugs distilled from native plants.

The juice of the maguey cactus, today distilled as tequila or fermented to make the poor man's drink, pulque, was widely used by the ancients. So also were tobacco, copal resin for its incense, and a wide range of hallucinogenic plants whose properties are only now being studied by modern pharmacologists and psychologists. There is, for instance, a seed called *ololiuqui* from which the ancients brewed a vision-inducing infusion. A plant called *toluah* of the datura family, is mentioned in the *Codex Badianus* written in 1552 by Martín de la Cruz, an Indian doctor; and there were various mushrooms including *teonanacatl*. The small tuberous cactus, *peyotl*, and the larger species of agave from which mescalin is extracted, have served Aldous Huxley and others for their experiments on states of heightened perception.

It has been found that *ololiuqui* and probably a number of other such drugs are chemically allied to lysergic acid, the most popular modern vision-inducing drug; so it would seem that modern chemists are beginning to catch up with the instinctive lore of pre-Hispanic Indians.

To the ancient Mexicans, plants yielding hallucinogens were sacred and god-given. The *Codex Magliabecchi*, which dates from just after the

conquest, shows an Indian eating a magic mushroom while the god of the land of the dead keeps guard over him as if showing him the spirits of those who have passed out of earthly life. Sahagún describes how, after having eaten and drunk vision-inducing drugs, the Indians gathered together to dance and sing for sheer joy. He lists dozens of divine plants used by the Indians to such an extent that in 1616 the Inquisition warned against the 'heretic perversity' of those who indulged in them, proclaiming that they received revelations through their use.

All intoxicating drinks, including the hallucinogens, were under the patronage of the goddess Mayahuel who was originally only a simple farmer's wife. One day she saw a mouse in a field and tried to kill it, but it escaped, making circles round her fearlessly and laughing at her. She noticed that it had been nibbling at the stem of a maguey plant, and that some cloudy sap had emerged. Mayahuel collected the sap in a gourd and took it home to share with her husband. As they drank together they became very loving and life seemed very good. So the couple introduced the pleasant beverage to the gods, who as a reward made Mayahuel goddess of pulque, her husband becoming Xochipilli, Lord of Flowers and also incidentally of gambling. A picture in the *Codex Laud* shows Mayahuel naked, seated on a shell shared by a serpent and a tortoise. Behind her is a cactus in flower.

Peyote and hallucinogenic mushrooms, whose properties were known to the ancients, continue to be used both for healing and for divination. The Huichol Indians of west Mexico regard the peyote as a divine plant, and at certain times of the year they make long pilgrimages in search of it. Woollen rhomboid designs represent the eye of the god, and magical drawings of animals and flowers, laid out in wool glued onto a board, are used in the peyote ceremonies. One, in my possession, has a stylised fish at the centre, circled by two snakes that are in turn surrounded by some kind of leafy plant – the whole suggesting that the creator felt himself penetrating down into the primitive fish-serpentine-vegetative part of man's nature to receive an unusually unified view of his own place in it.

Among the Indians so-called 'magic mushrooms' are said to be eaten

Xiutecuhtli as pictured in the *Codex Fejervary-Mayer*. It is believed that the ancient Mexicans, in their sacrifices to the fire god, made use of their knowledge of drugs to dull the sufferings of the victims.

only by special sages, who may nevertheless also prescribe them as a cure for certain illnesses; but a cult of them has arisen among some educated circles in the Mexican capital, and workers on their chemistry are watching with some uneasiness the possible results of bringing these ancient and obviously useful but powerful substances into the hands of sophisticated, often atheistic or at least agnostic pleasure-seekers.

The secret lore of the priest caste, which understood how to manipulate these drugs, was handed down from father to son, especially among a sect called the *Xochimalca*, or flower-weavers – that is, bringers of the godly state when the mind flowers into happiness. The use and abuse of halluci-nogens may provide a clue to the perplexing riddle of the degeneration of the ancient cultures; for it is evident that the religion of Quetzalcoatl, the original one of redemption and mercy, had become almost transformed by the time the Spanish armies arrived in the New World. The soldiers were not unnaturally horrified by the mass human sacrifices and the super-stitious adoration of a proliferation of gods and goddesses, some of whom appeared to be more properly demons. A genuine priesthood aware of its responsibilities and knowing that the ultimate purpose of inducing spe-cial states must be union with the godhead, would have been careful how they used their pharmacological knowledge. A degenerate priesthood could very quickly have discovered that the drugs gave them power, and would not have discriminated between evil and good.

For example, there was a herb called *petum* with analgesic properties if used as an ointment on the skin. Used in combination with an halluci-nogen, and by a man unable to distinguish between power and cruelty on the one hand, and power allied to virtue on the other, *petum* could become a sinister instrument. A Spanish chronicler called Acosta described how: '...by means of this ointment they became witches, and saw and spoke to the devil. The priests, when smeared with this ointment, lost all fear, and became imbued with cruelty. So they boldly killed men in their sacrifices, going all alone at night to the mountains, and into dark caves, not fearing any wild beasts because they were sure that lions, tigers, snakes and other savage animals that breed in the mountains and forests would flee from them because of this *petum* of their god... This *petum* also served to cure the sick, and for children; and so they called it the divine remedy... so the people went to the priests and holy men, who encouraged the blind and ignorant in this error, persuading them what they pleased and making them pursue their inventions and diabolical ceremonies...'

This is a far cry from Quetzalcoatl, who could not bear to hurt any living thing. But if priests had lost all sense of responsibility, the degener-ation is easily explained. As the idea of feeding the sun symbolically with 'hearts made god' became taken literally, so the use of special drugs would fortify the cruelty instead of acting as an adjunct to purification of the emotional life. The Nahuas knew the dangers that might arise when instruments of high knowledge fell into wrong hands, and a story about a poor rag-picker illustrates this. The rag-picker, who worked near the great temple of Huitzilopochtli, found a painted book that told him of a magic casket lying beneath the ninety-third step of the pyramid. It was impossible for him to move the stone alone, so he went in search of a priest, who agreed to help extract the casket provided the spoils could be suitably shared. At night they went together to the pyramid, brought out the casket which was bound by a silver chain, and opened it to find a magic rattle, a mirror that showed the future, a wand of power, a drumstick, and an almanac and book of spells. The priest knew how to make use of these objects, but the outcast rag-picker did not.

So the priest offered to buy the whole box for three hundred pieces of gold. As he was counting out the money, the rag-picker struck him on the head with the wand from the casket, killed him, and took him down to the river where he disposed of the body. Then the rag-picker set about trying to learn the mysteries, but without success. He was filled with fear because strange spirits seemed to play around him night and day. Disgusted with the casket and its contents, he tried to hurl it into the lake, but the priest rose out of the waters, snatched the casket, and then pursued the rag-picker back to the pyramid and killed him. The priest remained in possession of the casket, and one hopes that he used it thenceforth for more constructive things.

In our day a Spaniard, Francisco Guerra, now a research worker at the Wellcome Institute in London, has made a study of the drugs. He was lucky enough to have had the help of an indigenous Mexican botanist, J. Trinidad Pérez Nol, who helped him to gain the confidence of isolated groups of Indians. In a lecture given in London Dr. Guerra said:

'The consumption of up to ten or twelve *teonanácatl* mushrooms, after a period of slight muscular unco-ordination or inebriation, gives rise to a feeling of well-being and enjoyment, explosions of laughter, and the well-publicised coloured visions in three dimensions, followed by a deep sleep. Mazatec Indians still use it for divinations, but... doses of over fifty mushrooms are said to produce intense intoxication and permanent madness. Also when *peyotl* is ingested a feeling of well-being and visual hallucinations of a coloured nature are produced; some of them may be based in the remote past, others apparently cannot be related to any experience. Mental concentration is difficult, and external stimulations are transferred into mental hallucinations... Chemical variations in the molecular structure of mescalin suggests that the spectrum of action of these Mexican drugs can be enlarged and their action on the higher functions of the brain modified extensively.

'The rediscovery of this buried lore among the codices and ancient chronicles of Mexico and its pursuit both in remote Indian villages and in the laboratory has been an exciting adventure. However, the entering of this pharmacological legacy of the New World into the indiscriminating hands of Western civilization, unable to cope with its own drug problems of alcoholism and narcotics, must be regarded with apprehension.'

From Dr. Guerra's evidence it is clear that in ancient times any slackening or laxity among the users of hallucinogens could have brought about degenerate effects. But this was not always so, for the feast of mushrooms, which followed a 'feast of chieftains' and a 'feast of flags', was the supreme feast of revelation.

Sacrifice and humility

In any case, revelation was for the few who could understand the highest level of ancient religion. As we study the almost embarrassing plethora of myths of creation, it becomes clear that there are different levels among them. Some are closely related to physical fertility rites; others – somewhat confused and probably having reached us in degenerate form – present a harsh and not very attractive picture of a universe that is self-devouring and sternly self-perpetuating. Still others penetrate to the very essence of the creative process to emphasise its chief and most poignantly beautiful characteristics: its timelessness, its link with praise and adoration, and the need for sacrifice and humility if anything of value is to be attained.

Of all the myths stressing the sacrificial nature of creation, the most beautiful and complete is that of the creation of the Fifth Sun.

Left: an Olmec ceremonial stone knife from Villahermosa. A knife of hard stone was thrown to earth by the goddess Omecihuatl, and 1,600 heroes were born.

Below: a *macehual*, a young standard bearer of ancient Mexico. These youths were selected at an early age for religious rites, and could aspire to the highest honours in the state. Aztec stone carving.

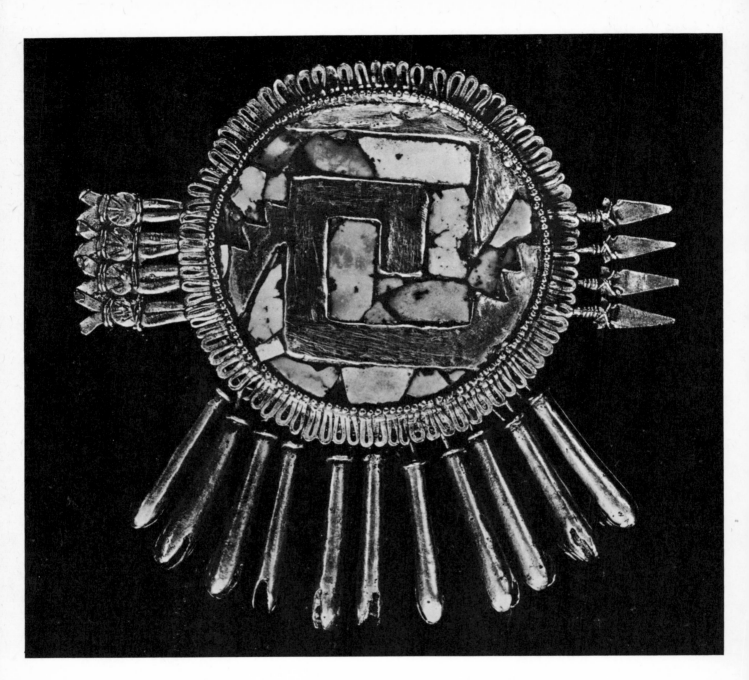

THE FIFTH SUN

A pectoral in turquoise and gold from the Mixtec tombs at Monte Albán. The round shield and horizontal arrows constitute the sign of war. The war god of the Aztecs was Huitzilopochtli, but in the religious sense he was also involved in the eternal, sacred war between light and darkness and the rising and setting sun.

Before there was day in the world – we are once again in that concept of timeless space – the gods met together and discussed who should have the task of lighting the new era. The gods' committee meeting was not unlike a human one; there was among them a braggart ready to come forward with an easy offer whose implications had evidently not been very carefully weighed.

A god called Tecciztecatl (whom we may remember as the deity of the death's head day, Miquiztli, and who later became acknowledged as the moon god) thought that perhaps he might earn some praise if he undertook what at first glance seemed a simple assignment – to give light to the world. But the other gods, being sceptical, or deciding that one alone could not bring to completion so vast a task, asked for a second volunteer. Nervously they looked from one to another, and each in turn made his excuses.

Only one god, to whom nobody was paying the least attention because he was afflicted with scabs, remained silent. Here, it suddenly dawned upon the rest of the company, was useful expendable material.

'Be thou he that shall light the world, scabby one,' they said, not very respectfully, to the god called Nanautzin; and he replied, 'In mercy I accept your order. So be it.'

Then the two – Tecciztecatl and Nanautzin – spent four days in penance. Thus prepared, they then lighted a fire on a hearth built out of rock. Offerings must be made at this solemn time, and Tecciztecatl's – as befitted a proud god – were rich feathers instead of dead branches; nuggets of gold instead of hay; thorns wrought of precious stones instead of those from the maguey cactus; thorns of red coral to replace those obligatory ones tipped with blood; and the finest quality of copal.

But Nanautzin, instead of branches, offered nine green reeds tied in bundles of three. He offered hay and maguey thorns anointed with his own blood; and in place of copal he gave scabs from his sores.

To Nanautzin and Tecciztecatl the other gods built a tower as big as a mountain; and within it the assembled company did penance for another four nights. After the bonfire had burned for four days, and after the receptacles in which the offerings had been made were destroyed, the gods lined up in double file on either side of the fire and facing it. They spoke to Tecciztecatl saying:

'Tecciztecatl, jump into the fire!'

Tecciztecatl made ready, but the fire was large and hot, and he grew afraid, and dared not throw himself in, but turned away. Again he made ready, but shied off. Four times he tried, and four times flinched, and failed to summon sufficient courage. As it had been decreed that nobody was allowed to make more than four attempts, Nanautzin was then called in his place:

'Oh thou, Nanautzin, try thou.'

Nanautzin gathered all his courage together, closed his eyes, and rushed forward blindly, casting himself into the fire. He crackled and burned like one roasting. Ashamed, Tecciztecatl followed the scabby god's example and threw himself onto the flames.

The lowliest of the gods had shown the way; and the Sun, which later was to be made the reason for a demand that men's physical hearts be torn out, owed its very life to a greater, voluntary sacrifice.

The unblemished youth

It should be evident that the voluntary sacrifice of life for the sake of redeeming the world is a very different matter from mass murder and the tearing out of the hearts of unwilling victims. The earliest human sacrifices in ancient America were probably voluntary. At one of the most important feasts in the calendar, for instance, that of the god Tezcatlipoca, a single youth was killed apparently with his own consent. This boy was taken to be the earthly image of Tezcatlipoca, and for a year before his death he was made the centre of extraordinary reverence, cherished and treated with the greatest respect. He was taught to play the flute, to fetch and carry the reeds and flowers required for offerings. He was taught to hold himself well, to be courteous and gentle of speech. Those who met him kissed the earth and paid him reverential bows. He was free to walk about by day and by night, but he was always accompanied by eight servants dressed like palace lackeys. His vestments were those of a god.

Twenty days before he was to be sacrificed the keepers changed his clothes for those in which he would end his life. They married him to four virgins who had also received a careful upbringing and who were

Praying hands carved from stone. A pillar ornament from the Gulf Coast region.

A Chac Mool figure from Chichén Itzá. The influence of the Toltec culture was strongly felt in certain periods of Maya history, and similar figures have been discovered in the great Toltec centre of Tula. They represent attendants of the rain god Tlaloc (or the Mayan Chaac) and these figures, adorned with shallow dishes to catch the rain, were carved to resemble the lumpy shape of floating clouds.

given the names of four goddesses. Five days before the appointed feast, honour was paid to the youth as to a god, there being much feasting and dance. Finally the youth was placed in a canoe covered with a canopy. With him went his wives, and they sailed away to a place where there was a low hill. Here the wives were abandoned, and now only the eight servants accompanied the youth to a small and poorly equipped temple. Climbing its steps, on the first of them he broke one of the flutes he had played during his year of prosperity and cherishing; on the second he broke another, on the third another, and so on until he reached the highest part of the temple where the priests were assembled waiting to kill him. They stood in pairs. Binding his hands and his head, they laid him face upward on the block. A knife of stone was plunged into his breast. It gouged out his heart which was offered immediately to the Sun.

The ceremony was a myth acted out in real life. The myth was about man, who must learn to glorify god through sensual things, through fine clothes and music and dance, before he is worthy of breaking the senses one by one and losing his life in order to gain it.

The deified heart

The sacrifice of the youth was linked with a profound philosophical idea that only the true, the deified heart is worthy to become nourishment for the great star that maintains life on earth. The Nahua peoples believed that we are born with a physical heart and face, but that we have to create a deified heart and a true face. The ordinary word for heart was *yollotl*, a word derived from *ollín*, movement. Thus the ordinary human heart is the moving, pumping organ that keeps us alive; but the heart that can be made by special efforts in life is called *Yoltéotl*, or deified. The phrase used to describe the face that we must make if we are to be truly men is *ixtli in yollotl*, which signifies a process whereby heart and face must combine. The heart must shine through the face before our features become reliable reflections of ourselves.

Thus heart-making and face-making, the growth of spiritual strength, were two aspects of a single process which was the aim of life and which consisted in creating some firm and enduring centre from which it would be possible to operate as human beings. Without this enduring centre, as the Nahua poet tells us:

> ...you give your heart to each thing in turn.
> Carrying, you do not carry it.
> You destroy your heart on earth.
> Are you not always pursuing things idly?

If we are unable to create this second heart and face, we are merely vagrants on the face of the earth. The idea of vagrancy is expressed in the word *ahuicpa*, which means literally 'to carry something untowardly' or without direction. There is another word, *itlatiuh*, which means to pursue things aimlessly. *Ahuicpa tic huica* means 'carrying, you do not carry it' – and this directionless carrying was believed by the Nahuas to be typical of man's ordinary state on earth. By accident we do not achieve direction, any more than we can be sure of travelling from London to Edinburgh by going to a station booking office and asking for the first ticket that comes to hand, or by thoughtlessly boarding the first bus that comes along because it happens to be moving.

But of course this idea of feeding the sun with a symbolic heart, created within a man's psyche, was very soon distorted. Offerings to the gods made in flowers picked from the meadows and the cornfields became offerings of enemy hearts torn out. As the friar Bernardino de Sahagún tells us:

'They used to make the prisoner climb on to the stone, which was round like a millstone. And when the captive was on the stone one of the priests... took a rope, which went through the eyelet of the millstone, and bound him by the waist. Then he gave him a wooden sword, which instead of knives had bird feathers stuck to the edge; and gave him four pine staves with which to defend himself and overthrow his adversary.'

In this way the prisoners were made to fight and kill one another, or alternatively the hearts were torn out by their captors. Either way it was the end of them, and the sun was left metaphorically licking its chops. The whole gory process is a long way from the Nahua ideal of creating the heart *Yoltéotl*, or of the Maya idea described by a modern student Domingo Martínez Paredez: 'One god who gave life and consciousness, and another who fashioned him, that is, who not only gave consciousness to man but at the same time formed and gave him human shape: only he had the virtue of being able to raise man above the other animals. So in Maya anthropogeny there exists the concept not only that consciousness is given to man, but also that it must be formed, and it is the gods' task to do this.'

This is the central idea and purpose of the Quetzalcoatl or plumed serpent myth, for Nanautzin is one manifestation of Quetzalcoatl. He is the plumed serpent in his lowliest state, but his self-sacrifice saves the universe from extinction and opens up latent possibilities not only for the heavenly bodies but also for man.

Tezcatlipoca, god of the smoking mirror, was patron of the knightly order of tigers (ocelots, the Mexican tiger). In this form he is pictured here, carved on one of the elaborate yokes which represented part of the accoutrements of the ball players. An unblemished youth was sacrificed, with his own consent, each year to this god. From Tajin, seventh to eleventh centuries A.D.

Overleaf, left: pottery figure of a seated Maya worshipper, probably during the month *Yaxkin*, which celebrated the firing of the fields to make ready for the new sowing. On that occasion all clothing and appliances were coloured blue and traces can be seen on the figure. The lips have been cut, probably in the offering of blood to the maize god Yum Caax. Late classic Maya, from Campeche.
Right: a barefoot Maya priest, modelled in clay. An example of the standard of pottery achieved in the culture centre of the island of Jaina off Campeche, which flourished about the sixth century A.D.

THE QUETZALCOATL MYTH

The side wall of the pyramid at Xochicalco, representing Quetzalcoatl as the plumed serpent.

The myth of the plumed serpent is dazzling in its beauty. It is the complete fairy tale. All things change perpetually into something else, everything is elusive, intangible, yet permanent and true. The great bird-serpent, priest-king Quetzalcoatl, is the most powerful figure in all the mythology of Mexico and Central America.

From Teotihuacán on the high plateau to Chichén Itzá in Yucatán and farther south, he is a dominant motif on ancient monuments. Sometimes, with his open jaws, bifid tongue, and articulated spinal column, he is misinterpreted and misused. In modern Mexico he frequently appears on friezes, mosaics and paintings that are as sentimental, as far removed from the originals, as Victorian Gothic from Chartres. What the Eiffel Tower is to Paris, what the lions in Trafalgar Square are to London or the Statue of Liberty to the U.S.A., even so is Quetzalcoatl to post-revolution Mexico seeking to re-establish its old traditions.

In the incarnate form which he is supposed to have assumed at a certain moment in history, Quetzalcoatl was a great lawgiver and civiliser, inventor of the calendar or Book of Fate. He was a compassionate king who, like the Buddha, could scarcely bear to hurt any living creature. Demons tried constantly to persuade him to homicide and human sacrifice but – as the anonymous author of the *Codex Chimalpopoca* tells us 'he would never

78

agree, because he loved his vassals the Toltecs, and his sacrifice was always of snails, birds, and butterflies'.

No one knows just who he was or whence he came. He therefore becomes fair game for every romancer, from D. H. Lawrence with his back-to-instinct philosophy, to others who equate him with Christ or turn him into a green and emerald Irishman. There are theories that he arrived in Mexico from Celtic lands or even from lost Atlantis.

Almost certainly there was more than one historical Quetzalcoatl. In ancient times the name was given to any priest who was supposed to have reached enlightenment. Laurette Séjourné, a French archaeologist living and working in Mexico, believes that Quetzalcoatl was a king living about the time of Christ. If it was he who discovered that maize was a good staple diet for human beings, then he must surely have existed much earlier. Carbon-14 datings show that maize was cultivated in the middle Americas about eight or nine thousand years ago. But the dates are tentative, some people having put them at eighty thousand years ago, which seems unlikely.

It is beyond dispute that a flesh-and-blood king did exist who was a great civiliser and lawgiver, an innovator in arts and crafts, and a man who stood high above his fellows in understanding and rectitude. So moral was he that he could never have condoned the human sacrifices that became, as we have seen, one of the central rituals in the religion of the Mexican high plateau. Such degeneration could scarcely have taken place quickly, even if aided and abetted by indiscriminate use of drugs. Therefore it can be assumed that the man Quetzalcoatl lived many centuries before the Aztecs, who arrived in Mexico at a late period, during the fourteenth century of our era.

A series of priests called Quetzalcoatl, however, adopted the name of the founder of their religion, and these were supposed to be 'perfect in all customs, exercises, and doctrines'. They lived chastely and virtuously, humbly and pacifically, comporting themselves with prudence and tact. They were supposed to be responsible, austere, loving and merciful and compassionate, friendly to all, devout and godfearing. This at any rate was the ideal pattern of the priest of the Mexican religion. That the truth often fell far short can be deduced from the bloodthirsty practices carried out in their name; but the first Quetzalcoatl, the man who created the myth, must have been of a different calibre.

Historically the facts are few. If we turn to the myth we shall see that it embodies a series of truths on different cosmic levels and which are in themselves ample proof of the existence at some time in the land of a great religious innovator. The Quetzalcoatl story exists: somebody must therefore have created it. If our aim is to study and understand it, it is really irrelevant whether the man who made it was the king of Tollan, as he is sometimes called, or whether he belonged to the civilisation of the Toltecs (master craftsmen) or to Teotihuacán (city of the gods) which is the site of the great Mexican pyramids; or even, eccentrically, whether he was Mediterranean or Irish or Chinese or, as some very respectable authorities have held, the apostle Thomas evangelising beyond the known world. The problem is nothing more than the hoary Bacon-Shakespeare controversy translated to Mexico. The question 'Who was Quetzalcoatl?' fades into the background as the myth speaks for itself.

To begin with there is the name, which has been analysed by Domingo Martínez Paredez. It is made up of *quetzal*, a rare bird with green feathers inhabiting the highlands of Chiapas and Guatemala, living in the tops of trees, seldom visible, and distinguished from other birds in having only

To hold the hearts of the sacrificed, *cuauhxicallis* or 'eagle vessels' were used, carved from stone and carefully decorated. The sides show eagle feathers, human hearts are represented on the rim, and signs signifying 'jewelled water' (blood) embody the idea of sacrifice. The glyph in the bottom represents the present universe. From Tenochtitlán, *c.* 1500 A.D.

The rain god Tlaloc scattering seeds. A prayer, or
incantation, is indicated by the speech scroll issuing
from his mouth. Mural painting from Teotihuacán,
first to sixth centuries A.D.

Right: a pottery figure of Xipe Totec from one
of the tombs at Monte Albán. He is shown here as
the supreme penitent, his face scarred in a line from
the eyebrows to the jaw and wearing a grimace of
pain. Zapotec culture, eighth to eleventh centuries A.D.

two front toes and almost no claws; and *coatl*, which is the Nahua word for snake but which is itself a combination of *co*, generic term for serpent or snake in the Maya language, and *atl*, the Nahua word for water.

From this derivation it is evident that the Mayas and the high-plateau Nahua-speaking peoples were in close contact by the time of the first Quetzalcoatl. The Mayas had their equivalent of Quetzalcoatl, who was Kukulcan but the curious thing is that the word Quetzalcoatl, the Nahua name for the god, includes the symbolism of the quetzal bird which belongs to the Maya lands and is not found on the high plateau. Both Mayas and Nahuas had erected a consistent, meaningful, and cosmically complete mythological figure who was at once water, earth (in the crawling snake), and bird. Quetzalcoatl was described as being the colour of jade or of some precious stone. He was the wind god, and also the god's messenger and road-sweeper. He discovered maize which allowed man – in the most mature sense of the word – to come into being. His heart was consumed by a bonfire which he himself built, whence it rose to become the planet Venus. His identification with the later Aztec sun god, Huitzilopochtli, gives him a claim to have passed beyond the planets into the solar world, source of life and light for our planet.

Quetzalcoatl was thus a composite figure describing the many orders of matter in creation: a kind of ladder with man at the centre, but extending downward into animal, water, and mineral; and upward to the planets, the life-giving sun, and the god creators. This ladder is very similar to the orders of matter and life described by the modern palaeontologist Pierre Teilhard de Chardin. It is not unsimilar to the seven powers of nature in Hindu philosophy. And it can be likened to Pico della Mirandola's Renaissance description of man: 'the intermediary between creatures, familiar with the gods above as he is lord of the beings below'. Quetzalcoatl is an embodiment of Mahommed's affirmation that God created the angels (stars, planets) and set reason in them, and He created the beasts (serpent) and set lust in them, and He created the sons of Adam (man, eater of maize) and set in them both reason and lust to war with one another until reason (Quetzalcoatl as king) prevails.

Quetzalcoatl's very name, then, seems to be a symbol of man's condition and of his possibilities. The story of his discovery of maize fits this general hypothesis. Man was not created until the gods had first bestowed upon him that special human food, sought and found by Quetzalcoatl, who stole the tiny precious grain that could transform the life of humanity. In the shape of a black ant, he stole the grain from the red ants; and maize became the symbol of manhood in all its fullness. The maize god Cinteotl is but another aspect of Quetzalcoatl.

Evidently the story of the discovery of food fit for men is more than a mere agricultural description. It is another expression of the ancient Mexican aim: to create a deified heart, and a face that shall be a true expression of the inner life of man. The temple to Quetzalcoatl, as described by Sahagún, must in its beauty have expressed the myth's inner meaning. It had four rooms; one all of gold and facing toward the east; one of turquoise and emeralds opposite to this, facing westward; one of sea shells looking to the south; and one of silver for the north.

The walls of another of the plumed serpent's temples were lined throughout with quetzal feathers. In this the room facing eastward was of yellow feathers; the western room was blue; the southern, white; and the northern, red.

Quetzalcoatl's physical description is recorded in detail. He was tall, robust, broad of brow, with large eyes and a fair beard, though there is at

Below and right: Quetzalcoatl, lord of life and death, depicted in an elaborately carved 'apotheosis' statue of the Huastec culture, *c.* 1000 A.D.

least one description of him that makes him black-haired. He wore a conical ocelot-skin cap. His face was smeared with soot, and he wore a necklace of seashells and a quetzal bird on his back. His jacket was of cotton, and on his feet he wore anklets, rattles, and foam sandals.

From a hill in Tollan his voice could be heard for a distance of ten leagues. In his time maize grew so tall that every cob was as strong and firm as a human being. Pumpkins reached to a man's height and cotton grew in all colours.

In so far as he was man, he was of the breed of heroes from whom myths are created. In so far as he is symbol, he presides like the wind over all space. He is the soul taking wings to heaven, and he is matter descending to earth as the crawling snake; he is virtue rising, and he is the blind force pulling man down; he is waking and dream, angel and demon (but in his demoniac form, as we shall see later, he is Tezcatlipoca). He represents daylight and also, when he journeys to the underworld, night. He is love with its transmuting power, and carnal desire that wears chains.

Life carries with it the possibilities of eternity and the threat of death, the seed and the flower and the fruit. Quetzalcoatl is time itself, the serpent, yet paradoxically he exists beyond time. With his coming he brings to earth the possibility of a miracle. One South American statesman – now many years dead – told a journalist who was searching for the solution to his country's problems that Latin America would discover and fulfil her true destiny only when the plumed serpent learned to fly. To Latin Americans with perceptiveness to catch the subtlety of the symbol, Quetzalcoatl's message remains valid.

In the Vienna Codex (*Codex Vindobonensis*) we see a naked Quetzalcoatl raised to the high heavens and receiving gifts from the Dual Lord and Lady above all. He is given four temples one of which is that of the morning star, his symbol. One belongs to the moon and is round in plan like the observatory at Chichén Itzá. The third is for healing, Quetzalcoatl's priests being called healers or physicians. Lastly, there is the temple of the knot of Xipe, only open to those of Toltec descent.

Among the gifts are a seed; a shell and a wind mask for the god of air; a spear-thrower and an arrow to give him power; a jewel and a feather-fringed shirt of the kind worn by high priests; a black feather with a pair of eyes, and Quetzalcoatl's distinctive conical hat. To the left, behind his naked back, are the mountain of the sun and the double-peaked hill of sunset and evening star.

From this heavenly plane Quetzalcoatl drops to earth by a ladder knotted like a sacrificial lash. Two gods follow him to the earthly regions. In Quetzalcoatl's hand is a staff sprouting life, and he also carries the spear of the morning star.

Like King Arthur of England, he is half man, half legend. His most enthusiastic modern devotee and student, Laurette Séjourné, believes that as a man he lived perhaps about the time of Christ; but, as we have pointed out, if it was he who discovered that maize was a fitting food for man, he must have lived many centuries earlier.

The name Quetzalcoatl, plumed serpent or water-bird-serpent, has also a secondary meaning: precious twin. The god's mythical twin, a dog called Xolotl (mythologically Venus as the evening star), may have derived originally from a Chichimeca explorer and king of that name; but the twinship theme has probably meanings on another level connected with the double appearance of Venus in the morning and the evening sky, and with the double nature of most of the gods in the pantheon under the dual god-above-all.

There are two main versions of the Quetzalcoatl legend. The first tells how the god-man fell from grace and allowed himself to be coaxed into a drunken orgy, during which he had sexual intercourse with his sister. When he recovered he repented, built his own funeral pyre, and rose to heaven as the planet Venus. The second version, according to Bernardino de Sahagún, tells how the great king Quetzalcoatl was attacked by enemies and had to flee from his lands. There follows a struggle between Quetzalcoatl and his arch-enemy Tezcatlipoca, whom we shall discuss later. For all its symbolic interest, Sahagún's version of the legend is of minor importance compared to the better-known story of drunkenness and transformation which appears in the Legend of the Suns.

Quetzalcoatl was born of Coatlicue, one of the five moon-goddesses; or she may have been a single goddess represented as a five-fold symbol, or quincunx, signifying Earth with her four directions and her centre. In her – as later in a different sense in her offspring Quetzalcoatl – spirit and matter fused. But whereas the fusion in the case of Quetzalcoatl allowed matter to be redeemed in spirit, his mother's function was precisely the converse: to solidify spirit into the tangible planet on which we live. Coatlicue thus made life possible, but not without the help of certain mysterious magicians and of the Sun. Until the magicians guessed the mystery of her existence, she remained hidden in cloud, alone and sterile. But when the Sun appeared to take her for a bride, all the instinctive forces of life came into being in Quetzalcoatl. Thenceforth Earth is both mother and myth; fruit and energy; seed and flower; gentle breeze and wrecking hurricane; loving caress and rending claw; stone and water. In her, through her son, the transcendent became tangible and coarse materiality took wing. Moreover, by becoming her consort, the Sun acquired new and unforeseen strength. Together with Earth and with Quetzalcoatl (as represented by the planet Venus), the Sun formed part of a trinity in which a balance and a concord was achieved. Sun was the male force impregnating the female Earth, and out of them was born a son, merciful and loving.

The statue of Coatlicue

If this description seems too kindly to fit the awesome statue of Coatlicue in the Mexican Anthropological Museum, we must remember that the statue is describing a vast cosmic process. Whereas it looks cruel to human eyes, it is aloof from either cruelty or compassion because it is describing an objective fact: eat and be eaten, for all will return to the basic skull form in death. A modern Mexican art critic, Justino Fernández, has described how humanity – mankind – is symbolised in the goddess's skirt of entwined serpents which hang from two creative gods forming the belt. In the skulls with which Coatlicue is decked we see the rhythm of life merging into death. Behind hang thirteen leather thongs encrusted with snails, and these are the mythical heavens on which rests the shield of Huitzilopochtli, the Sun god.

In the statue Coatlicue is clad about the thorax in human skin, to remind us that she is connected with Xipe Totec, the flayed god, god of spring. Her necklace of hands and hearts is a symbol of the sacrifice needed to maintain the gods and uphold the cosmic order. Two aspects of Venus are shown in the hands in the form of serpent heads, one being Quetzalcoatl himself, and the other his twin Xolotl.

At the highest point of the statue we find Omeyocan, the place in which the divine god-above-all lives with his consort. This is represented by a bicephalic mass which takes the place of the head and in a sense represents the Moon. Justino Fernández ends his description of the goddess: 'The

Left: a view of Uxmal from the summit of the House of the Magician, looking down on the quadrangle of the 'Nunnery'.

Below: the statue of Coatlicue, over eight feet high, in the National Museum of Mexico. The mother of the gods, she is pictured here as the description of a cosmic process rather than as a female deity. The statue was discovered in Mexico City on the site of Tenochtitlán, the Aztec capital destroyed by the Spaniards.

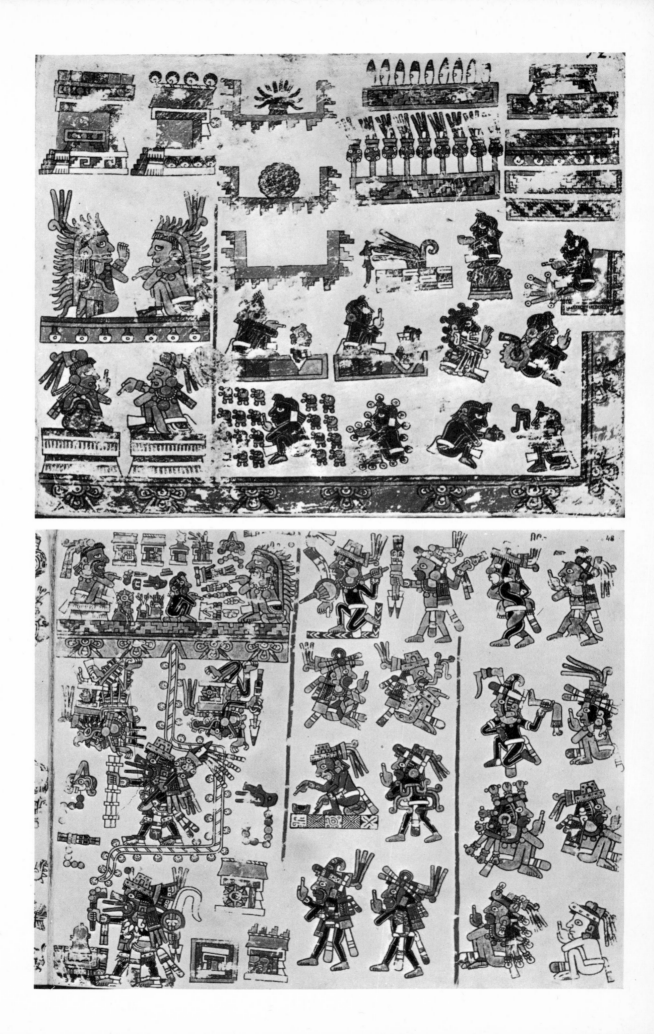

whole of her vibrates and lives, inside and out, the whole of her is life and is death; her meaning stretches in all possible directions... Coatlicue is the dynamic-cosmic force giving life and maintained by death in the struggle of opposites which is so necessary that its final and most radical meaning is war... Thus the dramatic beauty of Coatlicue has ultimately a warlike meaning, life and death; and that is why she is supreme, a tragic and a moving beauty.'

Tragic and warlike, one would add, only if she is looked upon with mortal eyes. On the cosmic level she is, like her statue image, a great pyramid or triangle representing stability and endurance.

Birth of the plumed serpent

Coatlicue, goddess of the serpent petticoat (as distinct from the goddess of the star petticoat, goddess-above-all), was both mother of the Sun and also the Sun's wife and sister. The suffix *cue* means petticoat and is a graphic word to describe a lady. One day Coatlicue and her four sisters, whose names are not recorded, were doing penance on a hill called Coatepec (Snake Hill – the name occurs as far south as Guatemala). Coatlicue, a virgin, gathered some white feathers and placed them in her bosom.

In another version the mother goddess swallows not a feather but an emerald – but the idea of something small and precious from which Quetzalcoatl arises remains. By this act his mother became pregnant and gave birth to Quetzalcoatl or Huitzilopochtli according to whether we are thinking in early Nahua or late Aztec terms.

In one dramatised version of the story, the goddess is called La, and she is alone, a widow, so she tells us, for her husband has died. As to her sons, they have gone away and live only in her memory, all four hundred of them. Then a feather announces itself, falling from the sky, lovely and soft and many-coloured. She places it in her bosom and begins to sweep the heavens so that her sons may come. All this appears to happen at twilight, a time when the Sun, her husband one supposes, has departed, but the stars, her sons, have not yet appeared. When night falls she lays aside her broom saying that it is useless to try to sweep night away. Sitting on the ground, she casts about for something to ponder, and remembers her feather. If she strokes it, she thinks to herself, perhaps the four hundred sons will come. But the feather is not there. It does not answer to her call. She begins to weep. Suddenly she becomes aware that she is pregnant and her face lights up with joy. She feels the baby quickening within her just as the four hundred had quickened before they were born.

In the next scene of the play the four hundred clamour to be told who has made their mother pregnant. Whoever he may be, they demand his death. The child, now sprung from the womb, declares himself to be Huitzilopochtli. As in the myth itself, he proceeds to kill the four hundred sons of Tezcatlipoca. The number four hundred, it is sometimes rendered as four thousand, need not be taken literally. It is used to signify the multitude of stars that are put out when the Sun enters the sky at dawn. On another level of meaning the number implies the diversity in the heavens that become unified by the birth of Quetzalcoatl-Huitzilopochtli.

In one version of the story the hero does not meet and vanquish the four hundred until he is nine years old. At that time the four hundred warriors who inhabited the Milky Way were filled with hatred against the boy's father – the Sun himself, though Quetzalcoatl is also the Sun. The anomaly fits the cosmic fact. Stars and Sun kill one another alternately as night follows day. So the four hundred killed the nine-year-old god's father and buried his body in sand. Quetzalcoatl was informed by

Left: two leaves from the *Codex Vindobonensis*. In the upper one the Old Ones, male-female aspects of the god-above-all, can be seen on the left. They bestir themselves and are manifest. To them, in the lower picture, has come the naked Quetzalcoatl. He is given four temples and the insignia of his various attributes, and returns to earth by a knotted ladder accompanied by two gods. At the bottom of the lower picture he can be seen wearing his wind mask (as the god Ehecatl) and his distinctive conical hat. He carries a staff sprouting life and the spear of the morning star. British Museum.

Below: a warrior, possibly a priest, decorated with plumes and flowers and with a characteristic Maya nose. The Mayas' ideal of physical beauty led them to flatten the head by tying boards to it in infancy. This head is from one of the tombs in the Temple of the Inscriptions at Palenque and may represent a priest of Kukulcan, the Quetzalcoatl of the Mayas. Seventh century A.D.

vultures of the murder; and with the help of a coyote, an eagle, a wolf, and an army of moles who bored a hole in the ground so that he could reach the skeleton, he recovered the bones.

Quetzalcoatl's temptation

As the boy grew up, evil magicians tried to tempt him to perform human sacrifices, but he would have none of this, being so filled with love toward all living things that he could not even be persuaded to kill a forest bear or to pick a flower. Then Tezcatlipoca, his chief enemy, showed Quetzalcoatl his image in a mirror. Quetzalcoatl was astonished to find his eyelids inflamed, his eyes sunken in their sockets, and his skin wrinkled. The face seemed not to be human at all, and Quetzalcoatl began to fear that if his subjects saw him thus they would destroy him. He went into retreat, thus conceding Tezcatlipoca the advantage.

Tezcatlipoca now decked his rival in finery so that he looked very splendid in a garment of quetzal feathers and a turquoise mask. With red dye he coloured Quetzalcoatl's lips, and with yellow dye he painted small squares on his forehead. A wig, and a beard of red and blue guacamaya feathers, completed the effect. When Quetzalcoatl looked into the mirror he saw so handsome a youth that he was persuaded to come out of his retreat.

The evil ones now tempted him with wine, but after a first refusal he dipped his little finger into the potion, and it tasted so good that he agreed to drink three times, then a fourth and a fifth. His servants followed suit, and soon they were all gloriously intoxicated. Growing ever merrier, Quetzalcoatl called for his sister, Quetzalpetlatl, and she too drank five times. The slippery path to carnal excess was begun; Quetzalcoatl and Quetzalpetlatl ceased to live ascetically and in cleanliness. They no longer pierced themselves with thorns, nor performed their daily rites at dawn.

But when the effects of the drunkenness had worn away, Quetzalcoatl repented and his heart was filled with sadness. He remembered his mother, the goddess of the serpent petticoat who ruled over the starry spheres, and it seemed to him that he was no longer truly her son. His servants grieved with him, until Quetzalcoatl ordered that he and his whole retinue should leave the city, and that a stone casket should be built in which he was to lie four days and nights in strict penance. This done, the pilgrims marched to the seashore; and there Quetzalcoatl dressed himself in his feathered robes and his turquoise mask. Building a funeral pyre he threw himself upon it and was consumed in flames. The ashes rose into the sky as a flock of birds, bearing his heart which was to become the planet Venus. It is said that when the morning star saw the birds fly aloft, it dipped down below the horizon to the region of the dead, and remained there for four days while Quetzalcoatl gathered arrows for his use in heaven. Eight days later he appeared again as the great star; and it is well known – says the myth – that since that time he has always been upon his throne.

The two Quetzalcoatls, mythical and historical, blend in a certain confusion. The myth of his virgin birth has several variants including one in which his mother swallows a sliver of jade. But all these events evidently happened both on the outer margins of history and somewhere in the high heavens. On the other hand at least one of the possible flesh-and-blood Quetzalcoatls was king of Tula, ruler over the Toltecs, and he lived during the tenth century of our era. But this was far too late for him to have discovered corn, and much later than early images of the god-man. Quetzalcoatl had by that time become a generic name for the priest-kings of

Tezcatlipoca, the god who brought about the temptation and fall of Quetzalcoatl. Aztec statue thirteenth to fifteenth centuries A.D.

Mexico; and the name derives from the symbolism of the myth, not from any one of the historical figures, whether existing at the time of Christ, or earlier or later.

The symbolism of the god

One of the chief clues to the meaning of Quetzalcoatl is to be found in the story of the creation of the Fifth Sun, for the humble god with his crop of boils is none other than the plumed serpent in embryonic form. This can be seen from the images of the humble god that appear in the codices always with the insignia of Quetzalcoatl – the very insignia possessed by the king of Tula.

The Fifth Sun was the sun of movement. Quetzalcoatl presides, therefore, over the era of movement – that is, over a period in history when the elements became fused, when 'burning water' came to represent the living spirit of matter in constant activity. The perpetual and necessary round of movement in the heavens which creates our day and night is represented by the passage of Quetzalcoatl as an eagle across the sky, his sinking into the underworld as an ocelot and his emergence again at dawn. But here, as in every aspect of the myth, we must be careful not to take the phenomenal meaning as the only one. The passage from sky to underworld and back is still another representation of the dark-light, spirit-matter dualism that so preoccupied the ancient Mexicans.

We have already touched on the triple symbolism of bird-water-serpent; but this needs further analysis. As bird, Quetzalcoatl represents the heavens, or the heavenly characteristics of man. Besides being associated obviously with his own bird, the mysterious quetzal so difficult to capture, Quetzalcoatl is often portrayed together with a humming bird which represented to the Nahuas the human soul released from its bodily scaffolding, sparkling in the sky and lighting upon whatever flower will provide it with the honey that is its pleasure.

Birds, however, are only one aspect of the god, for at a certain stage of its development the human soul must have a scaffolding or armature, in other words matter, which is symbolised by the god's serpent scales. In this aspect, as Laurette Séjourné has pointed out in an illuminating study called *The Universe of Quetzalcoatl*, the connection with the deities of water and of femininity are constant. Thus Quetzalcoatl connects with the great earth monster whom we have seen as a symbol of time and who is represented hung with the skulls of physical death. But it would be quite misleading to take this symbolism as implying any negation of material creation, for matter is an essential phase in the cosmic cycle and cannot be escaped – nor, if it were possible, would escape be desirable. It is precisely the 'movement' of the Fifth Sun that gives matter life and form and the glowing, jewel-like beauty of the myth. There is no question of denying natural laws at a certain stage in the soul's pilgrimage and transformation. The plumed serpent must learn to fly. In other words, matter must transcend itself and be transmuted into pure spirit. But so equally must the quetzal bird descend into matter and join with the serpent to become part of the whole instinctive movement of organic life. In other words, spirit must enter matter to infuse it with life.

The most solid matter is the most unchanging, and yet it contains, even in its immutability, the glow and brilliance of life. Therefore it is represented in the Nahua myth by jade, beads of which were placed in the mouths of the dead. Jade represents on the one hand inert matter which has not yet been infused with spirit, and on the other the deified heart which passes beyond movement to perfect stillness and which it is

A clay vessel in the form of a man blowing a conch shell, from Colima in western Mexico. The conch shell was one of the insignia of Quetzalcoatl, symbolising both his aspect as the wind god and – in the spiral – the growth of natural things.

to be hoped has been created by man on his journey through this mortal life. A notable characteristic of the Nahua symbolism is that it gathers opposites into one whole and thus shows us simultaneously the apparently contradictory facets of a single truth. The contradictions exist only because of our limited minds. On another plane stillness and movement, matter and the most illuminated spirit, the physical and the holy, all meet. Between inert matter and pure life there stretches a chasm bridged by the whole vast range of creation. Moreover matter and life, though at opposite poles, can look outwardly very much alike. Jade represents both.

So it is too with the symbolism of the flower. At a superficial assessment it would seem that the blossoms adorning Quetzalcoatl's headdress are the converse of the stone and represent growth and life rather than death and inertia. But flowers in much Nahua poetry remind us also that all created life on earth must perish. Life is ephemeral, we are reminded, and not to be made immortal unless the deified heart, the jade in the mouth, is formed.

For the most part flowers appear to symbolise a fairly high but still intermediate state of the soul on its journey upward to full godhood. There are wall decorations showing the blood stream flowing within the body of the serpent; and in the blood are painted flowers, as if within the god-man's blood something had grown and flowered but had not yet at this stage become permanent, as in the jewel or precious stone.

It is odd that with their constant reference to 'flower and song' the ancient poets scarcely ever specified particular varieties of growing things, though there is occasional reference to 'the cocoa flower' or 'the flower that makes us drunk'. The frequent mention of scent, though again never specifically, suggests that this was an important attribute of the plant, and it seems that in our day there exists in certain parts a very detailed 'scent lore', for the Guatemalan novelist Miguel Angel Asturias, in his *Hombres de Maiz* describes a 'pharmacy for concealing scent'. According to him, Indian warriors or hunters smell of their *nagual* or protective animal. In order to put their enemies off the scent when they are being pursued, they anoint themselves with a special aromatic water or with some ointment or fruit juice that will disguise the natural body odour. The root of the violet is specifically mentioned in this connection, together with heliotrope water for concealing the smell of venison. Even more potent are said to be spikenard, jasmine (against snakes), wild lily, tobacco, fig, rosemary, and orange water.

A central symbol in Quetzalcoatl's insignia is the conch shell, especially in its transverse section which in many stylised forms becomes the god's pectoral. As a transverse cut, it looks like half a star – half of the planet Venus to which Quetzalcoatl's heart was to rise. It can also look like the spiral so common in the growth of natural things, as d'Arcy Thompson showed us with abundant illustration in his *Growth and Form*. The conch holds sound and wind, and every child knows how, if put to the ear, it will reproduce the pulsations of surf beating on the shore. It is a fitting symbol for Quetzalcoatl in his role of wind god.

It is said that to ancient Mexicans the shell spiral represented birth; and Laurette Séjourné reminds us in this connection that Quetzalcoatl was the procreator of man, who endowed human kind with the special food, maize. What has not been pointed out is that the shell becomes a permanent record of the trace of its own growth. The chalky deposit of which it is made fixes the movement of growth's spiral so that we can see, in a single instant, the whole process from its tight, curled inception to its outermost whorl. It is thus a symbol of the permanence of time, of

An Aztec shield made of gold and feather-work, a fine example of a unique craft. The plumed coyote shows this creature's connection with the Quetzalcoatl legends telling how he helped the god recover the bones of his father from the underworld.

that space-time which is beyond either, which is eternal and unchanging, within and beyond the movement of organic life. In Nahua symbolism the shell represented the end of one era and the beginning of another, so that even permanence has its limitations. No time we can conceive of is absolutely unending, and all time is marked off by the passage of the great heavenly cycles. So the shell represents the relatively – not the absolutely – eternal. It is one completed cycle, visible and tangible.

The shell can also be the outer covering of hard matter within which the spirit is enclosed and from which, if it is to fulfill itself, it must at some stage emerge in splendour. The plumed serpent as man is he who seeks fulfillment whatever the cost may be. As Laurette Séjourné says: 'What makes Quetzalcoatl a king is his determination to alter the course of his existence, to initiate a journey to which he is forced only by inner necessity. He is the Sovereign because he obeys his own law instead of that of others; because he is the source and origin of *movement*.'

This is the central reason for Quetzalcoatl's existence as king and as god, and it puts him among the tiny band of the elect who, through all the ages have preferred freedom to bondage, immortality to imprisonment in passing time, lasting instead of transitory happiness.

Quetzalcoatl: Venus and sun

Significantly, it is the lower half of the transverse cut of the conch shell that is represented in the pectoral of Quetzalcoatl. His connection with Venus is very specifically with the planet when it dips below the horizon into what the Nahuas regarded as the underworld, or outer darkness. Quetzalcoatl was not pure divinity, not Ometeotl, the one god-above-all, but rather a god in the making, who had to 'descend into hell' and there suffer transformation. As a boy he penetrated into the underworld in search of his father's bones, which were rediscovered and thus revived by the son's persistence and with the help of those very earthy and instinctive animals – the wolf (or coyote), the tiger (or ocelot), and the mole. The eagle helped too, an indication that Quetzalcoatl would rise again on wings to heaven.

Later, when Quetzalcoatl had committed the carnal act and then repented, he had to descend for eight days into the stone casket, the underworld, before he rose into the sky. We have here on the one hand a physical description of the passing of the planet Venus below the horizon and its reappearance; and on the other a symbolic representation of a stage in the soul's pilgrimage.

The disappearance of Venus in the blinding light of the sun's rays suggests that the planet is swallowed up in the sun, becomes the sun – just as Quetzalcoatl is both Venus and sun. We see this aspect of his symbolism especially in his Aztec successor, Huitzilopochtli, who is the sun god demanding to be nourished on human hearts. In reality the hearts that Quetzalcoatl required were divine creations after the pattern of his own, purged and deified through suffering. It has always been a necessary part of the task of every religious teacher to help his followers to the same degree of illumination that he has reached himself. Thus Quetzalcoatl had to construct a bridge by which his disciples might follow him into the promised land. His message would have been nothing if he had not been able to teach others the art of creating a deified heart.

The twinhood of Quetzalcoatl is a complex affair. As Venus, his twin is the dog Xolotl (the word means both twin and dog); as sun his twin is a tiger or ocelot. Nevertheless, the passage both of sun and planet through the underworld is usually represented by the ocelot and not the dog.

The eagle and the ocelot (tiger) carrying standards and crowned with flowers. The orders of Knights Tiger was originally a caste of initiates whose purpose was the attainment of spirituality. The Knights Eagle were their higher companions, warriors of the sun. *Codex Borbonicus.*

The ocelot is the nobler animal and must be taken to represent a higher form. Quetzalcoatl as Venus in the underworld journey is less noble than when he represents the sun – or so one would think; and yet as Lord of Dawn (Venus) he is represented as the ocelot. Why? The ocelot howls at dawn to welcome the sun. Probably Xolotl represents the lowest bodily instincts, nonetheless necessary and nonetheless to be purified; whereas the ocelot represents certain higher instincts, or perhaps even the deepest feelings of man – feelings that cause so much trouble if they are not tamed and transformed. The ocelot, representing these higher feelings, must therefore pass through the underworld before being worthy of association with the redeemer, Quetzalcoatl.

The Mexican order corresponding to the Knights Templars of Europe was that of the Knights Tiger. It has often been mistaken for a warrior caste in an ordinary military sense. In fact it was a caste of initiates fighting for the attainment of spirituality. The special insignia of the knights was a thunderbolt, or flash of light illuminating man and his world; and their higher companions were the Knights Eagle, warriors of the Sun.

The Pochtecas

There was also a band of followers of Quetzalcoatl whose apparently humbler role was a decisive one in the society of ancient America. These were the *pochtecas*, or itinerant vendors who formed a guild or brotherhood with the material purpose of trade but with a central set of ethical principles that were more important to them than money-making. Wandering from their centre in Cholula near the Mexican capital, down into the Gulf lands and into Maya territory to the south, they were carriers of ideas as well as goods, and undoubtedly account for the enormously

widespread cult of their god and protector. They seem to have been hard-headed business men who were yet never allowed to accumulate wealth, their main mission being to search for the 'Land of the Sun'. They were transmitters of ideas. Quetzalcoatl s kingdom was not of this world but it worked within it, and very efficiently.

One poem in a lesser *Chilam Balam* manuscript (for the *pochtecas* had wandered as far as the Maya lands) makes it clear that their function was not merely that of salesmen:

> You are to wander,
> entering and departing
> from strange villages...
> Perhaps you will achieve nothing anywhere.
> It may be that your merchandise
> and your items of trade
> find no favour in any place...
> Do not turn back, keep a firm step...
> Something you will achieve;
> Something the Lord of the Universe will assign to you...

The *pochtecas* were closely linked with guilds of craftsmen, and all the guilds together may have had some inner teaching and purpose similar to the masons and other guilds of mediaeval Europe. That the *pochtecas* were highly esteemed is evident from the following poem:

> When the vendors reached
> the coast...
> the nobles who lived there presented them
> with great round jade stones,
> very green, the size of tomatoes;
> also jade, the colour of quetzal,
> emeralds like black water,
> turquoise shields,
> turtle shells,
> guacamaya feathers
> and others from a sea-black bird;
> and red tiger skins.
> When they returned to Mexico,
> they presented to the king Ahuitzotl
> everything they had brought.
>
> . . . .
>
> That is why king Ahuitzotl
> held the vendors in great esteem
> and made them equal to the knights of war.

Ahuitzotl was emperor of the Aztecs from 1486 to 1502. The *pochtecas* never made a show of their riches or power, but always behaved humbly. If they accumulated too much wealth, they organized religious banquets and quickly got rid of it. They were mysterious people in the ancient world, exercising their influence silently, behind the scenes, but acting as a thread binding the whole pattern of Nahua-Maya culture together and using coastal towns as centres from which to radiate their varied influences. Sahagún tells us that they had free entry into all manner of places, and that they were often afflicted by the intense coast heat and the lashing winds as they struggled to transverse mountain and canyon. He also describes their sacrifice of victims, but the esteem in which they were held makes us suspect that this was either a late aberration or an exaggeration of Sahagún's. Their god was Yiacatecuhtli, Lord of the Vanguard, or Nose and their own name means 'merchants who lead'.

Left: two Pochtecas, members of the guild of travelling merchants, from the *Codex Fejervary-Mayer*. They had a unique importance in the empire, being the only privileged class apart from the priests and the nobles. Their position might ultimately have led to the establishment of a true merchant middle class.

Left, below: Lord of the Vanguard, or Lord of the Nose, Yiacatecuhtli, from a pre-conquest manuscript. He was the particular god of the Pochtecas, the travelling merchants of ancient Mexico. As followers of Quetzalcoatl, they were carriers of ideas as well as goods, and helped to spread the cult of the plumed serpent over a widespread area. *Codex Fejervary-Mayer*.

The figure of Macuilxochitl, from a ceremonial vase. He was the god of games and feasting and an aspect of Xochipilli. Mixtec ceramic, from Miahuatlán in the state of Oaxaca.

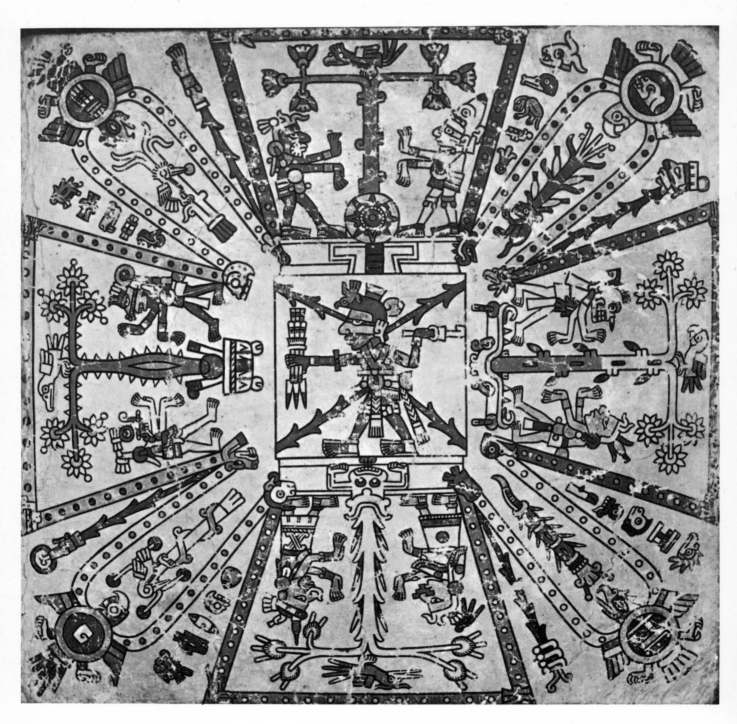

FOUR ASPECTS OF NATURE

The five world regions. A leaf from the *Codex Fejervary-Mayer*. At the centre stands Tepeyollotl, the god who was Heart of the Mountain and one of the Lords of Night. The four cardinal points were associated with the four sons of the dual god-above-all; Quetzalcoatl, Xipe Totec, Camaxtli, Huitzilopochtli. They were also connected with the four Suns which preceded our own world and ended in destruction. The fifth and central region was that of the present world and represented instability – Tepeyollotl was also the god who caused earthquakes.

At one time the Mexican gods who stood at the cardinal points of the compass were all Tezcatlipocas of various colours, though oddly the colours of the god do not seem to fit the normally accepted compass colours: white, north; red, east; yellow, south; and black, west.

Tezcatlipoca is black in his northern aspect, red in his eastern, blue in his southern, and white when he stands at the west. Later these four offspring of the one god-above-all and his consort became differentiated. The blue Tezcatlipoca of the south became Tlaloc, the god of rain. The red Tezcatlipoca belonging to the east, the point of sunrise, became Xipe Totec, the flayed god, or sometimes Tonatiuh the Sun itself. Quetzalcoatl was associated with the sunset, and Tezcatlipoca remained to rule the black land of the north. Alternatively Quetzalcoatl remained to conquer

94

three Tezcatlipocas at the other points. Each god represents an aspect of nature. It seems that in the land of the four directions beneath the great heaven there were three basic principles of nature more or less in constant warfare, or at least in opposition and collision which had to be resolved by the coming of the great humaniser and restorer of harmony, Quetzalcoatl. We can think of all four gods as Tezcatlipoca in various stages of the god-man's pilgrimage, or as Quetzalcoatl at various degrees of redemption.

(In parenthesis one might note that the four Tezcatlipocas had their Maya parallel in four Bacabs, also belonging to the points of the compass; but the Nahuas appear to have taken this idea of a quadruple 'compass-god' – in certain aspects possibly representing something very like the mediaeval 'four humours' – to a much higher degree of development.)

The idea of the four Tezcatlipocas standing at the four corners of creation is graphically expressed on a page of the *Codex Fejervary-Mayer* which has been neatly interpreted by Cottie Burland who regards the god as 'continually hopping round the pole star', prowling about some desirable centre but never able to reach it. In the Codex painting the centre is represented by the god Tepeyollotl, the Heart of the Mountain, one of the Lords of Night who ruled over part of the Aztec calendar. Around this figure the four Tezcatlipocas revolve. Curiously, however, while east is placed at the top of the page, north is to the east's right and not to the left as we would normally expect. Burland suggests that this is intended to be a night-time vision so that we ought to look at it as if we were lying on our backs and gazing upward at the sky. In contrast, the time sequence that occurs at the points of the square in the picture proceeds in the direction of the sun's apparent movement across the sky, from east to west (taking east as established by the night positions).

The topmost of the cardinal points can be identified as east because of its temple, which tells us that this is the holy place of the rising Sun. A quetzal bird is perched on a flowering tree. This is the holy land whence Quetzalcoatl arose. Two gods face one another: the god of the sharp-cutting stone, Itzli, and the god of the rising Sun. Throughout the picture we shall find this same preoccupation with dual forces in opposition. Moving now to the right we find, at the north point of the compass, the land of souls. Here Cinteotl, the maize god, faces Mictlantecuhtli, Lord of the Dead. The tree is rigid, contains a yellow parrot, and is decorated with what Burland thinks are bloodstained stone knives. They might equally well be hearts. Either way, the dual death-life theme is emphasised: knives that look like hearts, or hearts that look like knives, the god of resurrection meeting the god of death.

At the foot of the picture, at the western point of the compass, Xochiquetzal, goddess of flowers, is paired with a goddess of drunkenness and witchcraft. Beauty is set in contrast with ugliness. The tree is long and spikey and the bird perched in it is the humming bird.

At the southern point, to the left of the picture, there is a split tree. South is sometimes regarded as a place of redemption, and the split may represent the crack through which man can escape. The bird is white, and the figures are Tlaloc the rain god and an unidentified god probably of the underworld. Rain, necessary to the growth of organic life, is paired with the underworld where nothing grows at all.

At the corners, around these four Tezcatlipoca positions, are grouped various calendar signs. The sign *Acatl* is carried by a quetzal bird feeding on a white plant where a bird carries a seed in his back. *Tecpatl* is carried by a red parrot, and a yellow vine winds about a blue shrub on which

A Huastec statue of the god of maize, Cinteotl. Eleventh to thirteenth centuries A.D.

sits a yellow bird. The sign *Calli* shows a falling eagle eating the fruit of the tuna cactus, symbol of sacrifice. *Tochtli* carries a parrot, and a maize plant is being gnawed by a mouse.

Whereas the interpretation of details must be speculative, there can be no doubt that the growing, dying, regenerative and destructive contrasts in organic life were strongly in the artist's mind. This picture thus leads us to consider another aspect of Quetzalcoatl-Tezcatlipoca, embodied in Xipe Totec, god of spring, who in his ceremonial representations used to wear a human skin. Just as the seed breaking its husk and the earth's crust to emerge as a tender shoot must inevitably go through a period of struggle and of overcoming (though neither need be interpreted anthropomorphically, so Xipe Totec, god of spring though he might be, did not escape sorrow and conflict. He was the god who suffered his skin to be flayed in order that the active, growing principle hidden within matter could be freed. He is that same pustule-ridden god who redeemed the Sun. In other words, he is Quetzalcoatl as the stricken, humble redeemer, suffering – as Sahagún tells us – a series of diseases including smallpox and an eye infection.

When Xipe is rid of his pock-marked skin he can be clad in gold, symbol of pure spirit or light. Having passed through the epoch of penitence, he becomes Quetzalcoatl in his redeemed form. According to Sahagún he was worshipped by the Zapotec Indians of Oaxaca and the Tehuantepec Isthmus where men jousted and played happily in front of his temple.

The symbol of the growth of maize from the seed is one of the most important in ancient Mexican religion, as it was in the Greek mysteries. In the Maya *Popol Vuh* the creators are supposed to have needed maize for the making of man; and the grain was brought to them by four wild creatures: Yac, a forest cat; Utiu, a coyote; Quel, a parrot; and Hoh, a crow: 'And these four creatures brought the news of the yellow ears and the white... Thus they discovered food, and this it was that entered into the flesh of man created, of man made man. This was his blood, of this was man's blood made...'

Both Xipe and the corn god Cinteotl are important figures in the Nahua pantheon, and in the *Codex Fejervary-Mayer* there is a fourfold picture showing the varying fortunes of a maize plant and bearing a remarkable likeness to the Biblical parable of the sower. The pictures should be read from below upward, first the left-hand column and then the right. If studied in this order we see first a red maize plant burnt by the scorching sun. The soil is dry and the crop is being attacked by various birds including one with notes issuing from its beak. Underground an animal and a bird are burrowing, eating at the roots. This is the worst state of the sown seed, which dries and is attacked by enemies and has no resistance. The second picture shows the soil only half cultivated so that the maize plant produces only one ear. But even this gives reason to hope, and a jewelled god tends it. By the third picture we have entered the era of *ollin*, movement, the sign of the age of Quetzalcoatl as redeemer. However there is too much water, which prevents the maize from giving of its best. The rain goddess presides. In the fourth picture the soil is well tilled and the maize flourishes under the god Tlaloc who gives it just the right amount of water.

Tlaloc, god of rain, is the most benign of the four gods. In his purely agricultural aspect he is described by Sahagún as causing trees and plants to bud and flower and ripen. His face was painted with black, liquid rubber into which amaranth seeds were encrusted. His jacket was a net

A clay figure of a priest of the Mayan rain god, Chac, wearing an elaborate headdress. From the island of Jaina, seventh century A.D.

Right: a vase bearing the image of the rain god Tlaloc. Toltec culture, from Tula. Below: an Aztec clay cup from Cholula, probably for the drinking of the intoxicating pulque.

symbolising clouds, and his crown was of heron feathers. He wore a green necklace and foam sandals, and carried rattles, to create thunder, and a braided red pendant. Stylised images of him show large circular eyes that give the appearance of goggles, so that he is sometimes known as the spectacled god. Under various names, Tlaloc appears throughout Mesoamerican mythology. To the Mayas he was Chac; to the Totonacs, Tajín; to the Mixtecs, Tzahui; and to the Zapotecs, Cocijo. Whereas the energy most essential to life is wind, or Quetzalcoatl, the next is water, or Tlaloc. Both are essential.

Tezcatlipoca, whose favourite disguise was that of a turkey, and one of whose feet, amputated by the great Earth Monster, had been replaced by a mirror, was Quetzalcoatl's greatest enemy but not entirely a personification of evil. If we think of Xipe as the necessary struggle and the suffering in nature, and of Tlaloc as the reviving rain, whether violent or gentle, then Tezcatlipoca becomes not the personification of evil but rather the whole capricious unpredictability of matter which is at one moment heavy and inert, at another light and dancing. His mirror-foot is shaped like a rabbit curled up in the womb, and the rabbit, 'which jumps in all directions', is symbolic of unpredictability. Some say that Tezcatlipoca dropped from heaven on a spider's web, so light must he have been. He was god of sin but also of feasting. He rewarded good men and brought diseases upon the evil. He was invisible and impalpable; born out of cloud but nevertheless bringing to mankind the gift of intelligence. He could at a glance pierce stones and trees and even the hearts of men, so that it was possible for him to read our innermost thoughts. It was said that he had only to think of something and he invented it forthwith. Seats were placed for him at the corners of all roads. Men, it was said, were mere actors on a stage whose plays were designed to entertain Tezcatlipoca. The sacrifice of the virgin youth to this god was the culmination of a year-round cycle of festivities intended to placate all the conflicting forces in nature; but it is clear from the symbolism of the breaking of the flutes as the youth ascends the temple steps that the ceremony is a dramatic enactment of some inner process that man must undergo, and not merely a superstitious eternal offering to gods who were feared.

Sahagún's story of the struggle between Quetzalcoatl and Tezcatlipoca shows the latter to be a wayward god possessing enormous if unbridled power and able to control much of the destiny of man and of organic life. He was finally conquered by Quetzalcoatl but only after exacting trials of strength, and because of the latter's greater purity and loftiness.

It is said that Tezcatlipoca, having descended from heaven on his rope of cobwebs, transformed himself into an ocelot while playing a game with Quetzalcoatl, then drove the latter from Tula and pursued him from city to city until finally they reached Cholula, which stands close to Puebla on the road from Mexico City and was one of the chief centres of the cult of Quetzalcoatl.

There came a time when Quetzalcoatl's people, the Toltecs, fell into slothful habits and became an easy prey to the machinations of demons sent to bring their downfall. The demons are evidently all Tezcatlipoca, whose first appearance was as a crooked old man with white hair. Thus disguised, Tezcatlipoca offered Quetzalcoatl intoxicating liquor which, he said, would ease the heart and banish thoughts of death. Quetzalcoatl, sensing that his mortal time was ending, asked where he should go. To Tollantlapallan, Tezcatlipoca told him, where an old man would be waiting for him and where Quetzalcoatl would become youthful again.

The Maya god of sacrifice, shown on one of the great stelae at Copán in Honduras, c. seventh century A.D. His name remains undeciphered but he was probably the patron of the day Manik. His nearest equivalent among the Nahua gods was Xipe Totec.

Quetzalcoatl accepted the drink, said to have been made of the maguey cactus which today still provides Mexicans with the distilled tequila and the fermented pulque.

Although Quetzalcoatl had allowed himself to be tempted with wine, the disguise did not really deceive him, and the demon had to resort to a more indirect trick. Quetzalcoatl possessed a daughter whom all men desired, but he would give her to no man. One day in the market place she saw a stranger selling green chilli and with his sexual organ erect and uncovered. Sick with desire, she returned to the palace and so pined away that her father ordered the chilli-vendor to be found. A town crier was sent out, to no avail, for the man had vanished. It was only when the search had been abandoned that the chilli-vendor reappeared of his own free will, just at the spot where he had first been seen. He was brought before Quetzalcoatl, questioned, reprimanded, and ordered to cover himself with a loincloth; he replied that in his homeland it was the custom to go about naked. Quetzalcoatl accused him of having caused his daughter's illness and demanded that she be healed, but he answered, 'I am not the only man who sells green chilli.'

Quetzalcoatl continued to importune him. At his command, his valets dressed the itinerant vendor's hair, bathed and anointed him, and gave him a loincloth. Thus suitably arrayed, he was taken to the maiden and lay with her. Later he was acknowledged as Quetzalcoatl's son-in-law, and this angered the Toltecs. Still sure that the man was an enemy even though he had allowed him to be taken into the family, Quetzalcoatl did not discourage the Toltecs from doing battle with the impostor. To Quetzalcoatl's delight the Toltecs at first seemed to be gaining the upper hand; but the army of Tezcatlipoca finally conquered. Quetzalcoatl admitted defeat and went out to meet his son-in-law, announcing that the virile young man had proved himself and was now definitely accepted into the family.

So powerful was this Tezcatlipoca that for long he seems to have dominated the Toltecs. For instance, he caused them all to sing. From dusk to midnight they went on singing, taking the cue from his own lips; and the music was so vibrant and intense that many fell into the caves and canyons and were turned to rock. Like the children lured by the Pied Piper of Hamelin, the Toltecs seemed to become hypnotised, and could not imagine how such disaster had befallen them. They seemed to be without resistance to the forces engulfing them.

Time and again they fell into this besotted state until they almost destroyed themselves. Tezcatlipoca now took the form of a warrior and called all that remained to assemble in Quetzalcoatl's field of flowers. Without question the Toltecs did as they were bidden, and Tezcatlipoca descended on them and began to massacre them. Many were slain, and many were trampled to death as they tried to flee.

Altering his disguise once more, Tezcatlipoca went into the market place and began entertaining the people by holding a dancing figure of the god Huitzilopochtli (or Quetzalcoatl) in the palm of his hand. Many Toltecs crowded forward to see the spectacle. But Tezcatlipoca cried out to them, 'What kind of sorcery is this? Is it not just a ruse to make men dance? You ought to stone us!' So the Toltecs stoned the marionette-worker until the body fell, apparently dead. It stank, and wherever the wind carried the stench the common people died. Not until many had perished from the fumes did Tezcatlipoca – who of course, in true mythical and fiendish fashion, went on living quite independently of the temporary form he had assumed – ordered the body to be thrown away.

Overleaf, left: head and shoulders of a hollow figure in painted clay of Xipe Totec, the flayed god. Totonac style, from the Veracruz region.
Right: Tlacolteutl, goddess of childbirth and the mother of Cinteotl and Xochiquetzal. This figure probably shows the birth of one of these. In another aspect she was the goddess of carnal sin – but as the 'Eater of Filth' she consumed the sins of mankind, receiving confession of their misdeeds. This was rewarded with total absolution but could only be made once in a lifetime. Aztec statuette with garnet inclusions.

A wooden mask covered with turquoise mosaic. The fangs suggest that it was a cult object associated with the Jaguar caste and probably used in religious rites. Very few exist; most were hidden from the Spaniards and the secret of their whereabouts subsequently lost. Mixtec, from Tilantongo, eighth to eleventh centuries A.D.

The Toltecs put a rope round the body and sought to drag it out of the city; but is was so heavy it would not budge. The corpse to which they had at first paid no attention and which they had believed unimportant turned out to be their greatest trial. Even when a town crier was sent out for more assistance, nothing could be done against the weight of the stinking corpse. And all this time the Toltecs behaved as if drugged.

Next Tezcatlipoca caused a white kite, its head pierced by an arrow, to fly to and fro as an evil omen over the heads of the Toltecs. He also caused a volcanic eruption. A mountain is said to have burned and stones to have rained down upon his enemies. Later still he became a little old woman selling paper flags among the crowds. Those who asked to buy one were sent immediately, at Tezcatlipoca's orders, to the sacrificial stone; they did not protest, nor could they help themselves for they were 'as if lost'.

Finally, after all the food had turned acrid and people were in danger of starving, an old woman came and began toasting delicious maize which sent out such a fragrant scent that crowds appeared from the most remote places to taste it. All the Toltecs left alive were now gathered in one place, so she – or rather he, for the old woman was Tezcatlipoca in disguise again, as we might have surmised – was able to go among them and slay them all.

The first trial endured by Quetzalcoatl is evidently a test of his power to overcome sensual pleasures, symbolized by wine. After that comes the temptation of sex, which is not suffered by Quetzalcoatl directly but by his daughter, and which finally puts all the Toltecs into a state of stupor. Then comes the desire for glory in battle, which Tezcatlipoca makes use of in order to lure the Toltecs to the 'field of flowers', a field of glory. After this comes an interesting trial, depending upon whether the Toltecs will be persuaded to mock even their own god Quetzalcoatl. They actually enjoy the degrading spectacle when he becomes Tezcatlipoca's plaything. It is only when Tezcatlipoca himself orders them to stone the marionette-worker that they do so, and then the result is disastrous, a stinking burden none can move. The besotted, drugged condition of Quetzalcoatl's followers goes from bad to worse, until they are unable to detect the evil quality in the fragrant maize brought them by an enemy. The very food given to them by their god Quetzalcoatl, as being fitting sustenance for man, becomes their downfall.

The departure

With his subjects all slain by the woman who brought them the fragrant maize, Quetzalcoatl decided finally to abandon Tula. He burned his houses of gold and coral and hid away all his treasures in the canyons and mountains, changing the cacao trees into dry mezquite fit for the desert, and sending the birds away. Taking the road, he and his remaining subjects set out for Anáhuac, the 'place at the centre, in the midst of the circle'. In other words, they now began their pilgrimage back to the source and inspiration of their being – the other holy place of the Toltecs, Tula, having become untenable.

They reached a spot where there was a stout, tall tree. Calling for his looking glass, Quetzalcoatl inspected his face and saw that he was now an old man, and he hurled stones at the tree, where they remained embedded in the trunk.

Flute players accompanied him as he proceeded forward. He rested on a stone and wept; hailstones rolled down his cheeks and gouged holes out of the stone, which also received the imprint of his hands and buttocks. Coming to a broad, long river, he laid stones to make a bridge, and after crossing over he came to a spot guarded by devils who sought to urge him back. But Quetzalcoatl said, 'I must go to Tlapallan, for I go to learn.'

'What wilt thou do?' the devils asked him, and he answered, 'I am called hence. The Sun calleth me.' They told him he would be allowed to go on condition that he left all his famous craftwork behind. They wrested from him all his skills; the casting of gold, the cutting of precious gems, wood carving, stone sculpture, the knowledge of the scribes and the art of feather work. At last in despair Quetzalcoatl cast his personal jewels into the water. Evidently in order to reach the place where he would 'learn' it was necessary for him to be deprived of this world's riches and of the crafts he had taught to his subjects. He must arrive poor. He encountered yet more devils, and when they accosted him replied that he was on his way to Tlapallan in order to learn. One devil tempted him with wine, but Quetzalcoatl refused until the devil insisted that nobody was allowed to proceed beyond that spot if he did not become drunk and stupefied. So Quetzalcoatl drank the wine, and fell asleep by the roadside, thundering as he snored.

Waking, he set off once again, and climbed the two snow volcanoes Popocatépetl and Ixtaccíhuatl, leading all the dwarfs and hunchbacks up

The growth of maize. Reading from right to left; the water goddess Chalchihuitlicue provides too much abundance, then the seed struggles with the harshness of a dry soil, manifest in the god Tepeyollotl who was Heart of the Mountain. Next the rain god Tlaloc brings the life-giving water in the right amount and, finally, the seed breaks through – Xipe Totec – and flourishes. *Codex Fejervary-Mayer.*

Bottom left: the rain god of the Zapotec culture was called Cocijo, represented here in a funerary urn from Monte Albán. Clay, ninth to fourteenth centuries A.D.

Xolotl, twin brother of Quetzalcoatl, represents
the planet Venus as the evening star. This Aztec
jadeite carving shows him as the death spirit on the
obverse, while the reverse carries the sun, which
dies at the rising of the evening star.

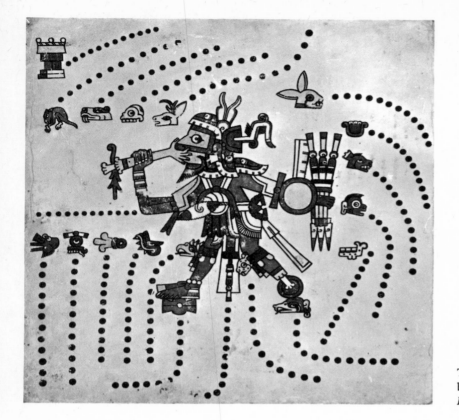

Tezcatlipoca eating flesh. The smoking mirror can be seen behind his ear in this leaf from the *Codex Fejervary-Mayer*.

the mountain until they died of cold. The dwarfs must have been a great loss to Quetzalcoatl, for in Mexican mythology they represent the tiny creatures of great power that we find in legends all over the world – the ants, the Tom Thumbs, the little fairies who do good deeds for people unseen. Veneration of dwarfs extended to Yucatán, where a small temple at Uxmal is known as The Dwarf's House. It is said that an old woman found an egg which she wrapped in cotton cloth and placed in a corner of her hut. One day the shell broke and a tiny mannikin crawled out. He went to court, and challenged the monarch to a trial of strength. The monarch asked him to lift a heavy stone, which he easily did. Vexed, the monarch then ordered him to build a palace taller than any in the city. Next morning there it was, for the mannikin turned out to be a sun dweller born of a cosmic egg.

No wonder then that on losing his dwarfs Quetzalcoatl wept and sang to himself as he gazed across at the third snow mountain – the one now called Orizaba but known in former days as Citlaltepetl. Elsewhere he planted maguey, and built a ball court with its stone ring, and shot at two silk-cotton trees and pierced them. He built a house in Mictlan, Land of the Dead. He proved his strength by pushing with his little finger a great rock that no other man had been able to budge from its place. And finally he set off on his raft of serpents to an unknown destination. The question has been asked, 'Why a raft of serpents?' Perhaps it was because he had conquered time and the lower ranges of the body.

Thus did the plumed serpent, Quetzalcoatl, triumph over the lord of the noumenal world Tezcatlipoca. Not without a struggle. Not without near defeat. But proving in the end the force of spirit over the illusory or only partially 'real' world of matter. Tezcatlipoca, sprightly, elusive, ever-changing, wore sandals of obsidian to show how firmly he was based on matter; whereas the wind-god and redeemer Quetzalcoatl had white sandals which – when interpreted together with the rest of his symbolism – may be taken to mean that wherever he trod he purified.

Characteristics of Tezcatlipoca

There was a statue of Tezcatlipoca said to have been of black stone like jet and to have been covered with gold and silver sequins. From the lower lip hung a glass bead in which was encased a green and blue feather which at first sight looked like a jewel. His hair was tied with a golden band, his headdress was of quail feathers, and he wore golden earplugs tinted with smoke to represent the prayers of the afflicted (whispered to him, presumably, in the intimacy of some Nahua confessional). From his neck hung a golden pectoral and he wore gold bracelets on his arms. An emerald marked his navel. In one hand he held a fly-whisk made of precious feathers, or else a spear; and in the other a shield and four arrows. In a disk burnished like a mirror he was able to see all that went on in the world. His stone was obsidian (*tezcat* means obsidian) used as late as the eighteenth century by Nahua-speaking Indians who regarded it as one member of a trinity together with the serpent and the dawning sun.

Sometimes he was represented seated in front of a red curtain on which were painted skulls and bones. He ruled over night and was in one aspect the Moon. The jaguar was his anvil, and he sometimes cried out like a bird of foreboding.

Tezcatlipoca presided over the school of plebeians, whereas Quetzalcoatl was patron of the academy of nobles where the army leaders, priests, and judges of the Aztec-Nahua establishment were trained. Tezcatlipoca is thus more immediately popular and human, less aloof than Quetzalcoatl. His smoking mirror, together with another opaque disk replacing the foot amputated by the earth monster, showed that he belonged to the world of noumena, the clouded world of half-perception and half-truth. In a sense he was a necromancer (and in that guise he tempted Quetzalcoatl), and he had some affinity with the Maya god Huracán whose very name suggests great energy unleashed and uncontrolled.

Tezcatlipoca sowed discord, but in a mischievous and not in a malevolent sense. He stimulated sexual activities but also received the confessions of lovers and others. He was lord over the material possessions of this world, and he could at will dispense or withhold them. He was a friend of the powerful, but also of slaves who were the humblest members of the community. Even more significant, those born under his sign were not ruled by fate but could be happy or accursed according to what they themselves were able to make of their inheritance.

It seems, therefore, that Tezcatlipoca, far from being a satanic figure, represented a kind of neutral energy. Like electricity it flowed freely and untrammeled, ready to be tapped and used, or wasted and left dangerously unharnessed, according to the individual whim, or the individual capacity, of each man who came under his power. The myth shows, like electricity, an interplay of positive and negative forces. Thus Quetzalcoatl was vanquished by Tezcatlipoca, and passed beneath the earth, and was again reborn; and in his rebirth he conquered his conqueror so that Tezcatlipoca's fate was finally to fall in a cascade of star-dust: the stars visible in the night sky. Although he was Lord of the Smoking Mirror, if the mirror were used as it ought to be it could reflect all the beauties of nature. In his breast there were two little doors meeting at the centre. A brave man might be able to open them and take hold of the heart within, in which case he was allowed to ask from Tezcatlipoca whatever ransom he chose; but any weakling who challenged Tezcatlipoca and failed to reach his heart would certainly die.

He is sometimes called the god of fire, although there was another god of fire in his own right – Xiuhtecuhtli also called Ixcozauhqui, of the yellow

face. Tezcatlipoca's paradoxical nature is never more clearly underlined than when we find him falling in love with Xochiquetzal, goddess of flowers and love, who lived on a mountain top surrounded by dwarfs, musicians, and dancing maidens, and who enticed all men by her charm. Tezcatlipoca snatched her from her true husband, Tlaloc. Tenderly Tezcatlipoca sang of her:

> She seems to me indeed a very goddess,
> she is so lovely and so gay.
> I must catch her, not tomorrow nor any time after
> but now in the very instant;
> I myself in person order and decree it shall be so.
> I, the warrior youth, shining like the sun
> and with the beauty of dawn.

Tezcatlipoca recognised that to achieve one's aim, to win the most precious thing in life, it is essential not to delay a single moment but to act forthwith. He also felt instinctively that beauty merits beauty, that he – so handsome as to be likened to the dawn – was destined for the flower goddess, lovely and gay.

Tezcatlipoca had thus a direct link with the merriest deities in the Nahua pantheon. Flower and song represented the words of the gods, manifest to mankind only through revelation. The deities of flower, dance, and games were precisely Xochiquetzal and her male twin Xochipilli. They were particularly closely associated with the later Aztec representation of Quetzalcoatl – Huitzilopochtli. At the feast of the flower gods, a bower of roses was built in Huitzilopochtli's temple. Here Xochiquetzal was

A ceremonial axehead – *hacha* – representing a warrior wearing an eagle headdress. The eagle represented the powers of light. From Itzapa, Guatemala, seventh to ninth centuries A.D.

Left: a gold pendant found in Tomb No. 7 at Monte Albán by Alfonso Caso. The disk represents the sun; above it are two ball players on either side of a serpent head. Below the disk is a moon glyph, followed by a representation of the Earth Monster which was seized by Tezcatlipoca and Quetzalcoatl. A fine example of Mixtec art, eighth to eleventh centuries A.D.

enthroned, and youths masquerading as birds and butterflies danced about her and climbed the artificial trees that had been erected for the occasion.

One version of the flower goddess story is that a flood destroyed all creatures except a god called Coxcox or alternatively Teocipactli and the goddess Xochiquetzal. The couple had many children, all of whom were born mute until a dove living in a high tree gave them each a voice and a different language.

Butterflies were particularly associated with Tezcatlipoca transmuted – in other words with Quetzalcoatl. In Teotihuacán, where a palace has been discovered evidently belonging to the priestly caste dedicated to Quetzalcoatl, there is a frieze showing the god's first entry into the world in the shape of a chrysalis, out of which he breaks painfully to emerge into the full light of perfection symbolised by the butterfly.

A Nahua triumvirate

On one side of his neutral but always ebullient nature, Tezcatlipoca links with song and flowers and butterflies; on the other with wickedness and sin. He is the direct opposite of Itzlacoliuhqui, the god of the curved obsidian knife (which also represents Tezcatlipoca himself so that Itzlacoliuhqui and Tezcatlipoca are sometimes taken to be one). Itzlacoliuhqui, god of ice and blindness and cold and obstinacy, represented matter in its most inert state, dead and immobile; and Tezcatlipoca that spark which gives uncontrolled, undisciplined vitality to stone and flower. Quetzalcoatl, making in this context a third in the triumvirate, is the saviour of a situation that, if left to itself, can lead to grave dangers, to chaos, and even to crime. He is the inspirer of values, of direction, and of discipline.

In the *Codex Cospiano*, Itzlacoliuhqui is seen making an offering to the powers of darkness, at the base of whose temple there is a human heart torn out. Inside it sits Tlacolotl, the great horned owl, omen of deepest evil. He represented to the Nahuas something far worse than the ordinary owl, who is merely the harbinger of death. Terrible as Tlacolotl is, however, the fumes that rise from him cannot obscure the sun which shines nevertheless. As Itzlacoliuhqui offers him a dark cloud of incense, blood flows from the god's self-mutilated ears. Like a fallen angel, this god had been cast down from heaven and blinded, so that on earth he was said to strike indiscriminately at his victims like the blind Greek fates. In the picture, his jaguar-skin mouth identifies him also with Tepeyollotl, Heart of the Mountain or of earthquakes; and by the same token he walks on lava rock. His evil appears to be that of material calamity, and not the more insidious evil of inner corruption, represented by certain female deities we shall refer to presently.

This god had his feminine counterpart, Itzpapalotl – the obsidian butterfly, the soul in the most permanent form, crystallised into rock. So the god of the sacrificial knife is also the soul god, for soul-making requires sacrifice of our lower natures. Perhaps because the soul is invisible, men cannot see Itzpapalotl entire, but only her jaguar claws. She seems to represent those delights that man, fallen from grace, has been deprived of; for there is a story that one day while picking roses in a garden she pricked her finger. Blood having once been caused to flow, she was obliged to deprive man of his happy pleasure-ground. But she may also be said to have fallen in another sense, for obsidian (the soul) was believed to have dropped from the stars. Obsidian is very important in ancient symbolism, and there is one story of the goddess of creation giving birth to an obsidian knife from which sprang sixteen hundred demi-gods who peopled the earth. Maize is often pictured in the form of an obsidian knife

Left: the Lord of the Region of Death portrayed on a remarkable piece of Mixtec gold work. This pectoral ornament shows Mictlantecuhtli with an elaborate headdress and there are two dates recorded on the breast pieces. He presided over the northern regions as well as over the hells below the earth. Eighth to eleventh centuries A.D.

The Plumed Serpent, god of learning, the planet Venus, great sky god – Quetzalcoatl was also the culture hero of the ancient Mexican peoples and a king of that name who ruled the Toltec people of Tula. He was also a great god of the Mayas. Aztec carving, thirteenth to fifteenth centuries A.D.

Xilonen, goddess of the young corn, and female counterpart of Cinteotl. Aztec carving.

and obsidian was often connected with lightning; it was the drak mirror of Tezcatlipoca, whereas Quetzalcoatl is rather connected with greenery and with jade.

In these three gods – Quetzalcoatl, Tezcatlipoca, and Itzlacoliuhqui-Itzpapalotl – we can see the different states of creation, always moving, always changing, always dying and being reborn. As the late Paul Westheim, a loving student of Mexican art, pointed out, life perishes but the energy of life is indestructible. The universe is composed of dynamic forces that are at once destructive and creative. The clash of such forces creates all cosmic events, and their interaction creates the world of nature. In this play of forces one against the other, all physical phenomena – not only man but even the stars in the sky – sooner or later die. But the vital energy (which we may surely equate with soul, obsidian) continues independently of space, time, and matter. It is the vital energy that is real: nothing else. Material things are mere appearance, simply one of the forms this energy can assume. Everything that exists is changing constantly; and change itself, life, is eternal.

According to Westheim, this idea of the constant clash of forces, of change on one level and constancy on another, is a fundamental concept of precolumbian thought. We find it expressed everywhere in the myths, particularly in the clashes between Quetzalcoatl and Tezcatlipoca. We find it also in the symbolism of eagle and tiger (ocelot) – the latter representing the powers of darkness and the underworld, the former of light. The knightly Orders of Eagles and Ocelots express the same inherent struggle in nature, and both are in a sense equally important. Light cannot exist without darkness, nor darkness without light. Man triumphs when he accepts and goes along with the contradictory forces in his nature, not when he tries to impose upon them some kind of artificial logic.

Yielding to the forces of nature

The idea of yielding to the forces of nature is contained in the parallel roots of the words *atlatl* (arrow), and *atl* (water). Atlaua, an obscure god, is known as the 'master of waters', but he is also associated with arrows, and he sings: '...I leave my sandals behind. I leave my sandals and helmet... I cast off my arrows, even my reed arrows. I boast that they cannot break. Clad as a priest, I take the arrow in my hand. Even now I shall rise and come forth like the quetzal bird.

'Mighty is the god Atlaua. Truly I shall arise and come forth like the quetzal bird.'

Armed with arrows, by derivation soft as water and thus unbreakable, this god needs no helmet. Armed only with reed arrows he can emerge as the quetzal bird, the holy symbol of regeneration. Thus is duality eventually conquered.

We find duality again in the concept of the Moon god-goddess presiding over both the death and the regeneration of plant life on earth. Moon rules the drunken man asleep, and also his awakening; the human being hypnotised into a soporific state when he has no control over his actions, and at the same time the awakened 'man made man' who is lord over creation on earth. The Moon – Tecciztecatl, was observed by the Nahuas in all his contradictions. They saw how, when he first appeared he was 'like a bow, like a bent straw lip ornament, a very tiny one. He did not yet shine'. Slowly he grew larger until after fifteen days he was quite plump, and then he appeared in the Sun's place. When the night sky darkened he appeared 'like a large earthen skillet, very round and circular, seeming to be a bright, deep red. And after this, when he was already

The image of the plumed serpent, Toltec-Maya style. From the Temple of the Warriors at Chichén Itzá. The figure above is a standard-bearer.

some way on his travels, when he had risen, he became white'. It was said, 'Now he puts out moonbeams.' Then, so it was noticed, something that looked like a rabbit appeared on his face. If it was cloudless, not overcast, he shone like the Sun and it seemed to be day.

Then little by little he grew small again, becoming as he had first appeared, waning and vanishing. It was said, 'The Moon sleeps soundly now, falls into deep sleep. It is already near morning, near daybreak when he rises.' When he had vanished completely the Nahuas said, 'The Moon has died.'

There is a sequel to the story of the humble god Nanautzin who with the reluctant Tecciztecatl saved creation by burning himself up and thus allowing Sun and Moon to continue (Nanautzin as Sun and Tecciztecatl as Moon). The gods while playing with the two stars (at first they were both suns), struck Tecciztecatl's face with a rabbit, maiming and dimming him, so that thenceforth he was Moon.

It was necessary to bow before these cosmic facts, to yield to them, to go along with them. But it was not always easy, and at eclipses of either Sun or Moon there was profound fear and much weeping lest the powers of darkness should overcome the world. At an eclipse of the moon especially, it was thought that unborn children might be turned into mice. Women placed obsidian in their mouths so that their children would not be born deformed.

Tonantzin, the Aztec goddess of motherhood. There is a shrine to the Christian mother of god near Tenayuca on the very site where in ancient days the Mexicans worshipped this deity. Aztec basalt carving, with eyes of mother-of-pearl.

SOME FEMALE DEITIES

Strangely enough it was sometimes the female deities who personified cruel and evil forces, the darkest side of nature. The great mother goddess, it is true, was the patron of physicians, midwives, and owners of steam baths. From the liquid rubber on her lips and the circles of rubber on her cheeks we might think that she bore some relation to Tlaloc; but she was also decorated with flowers and a shell-covered petticoat, and she carried a broom, all of which suggests that she may have been a kind of female equivalent of Quetzalcoatl, wind-god and road-sweeper of the gods. There was another goddess more closely associated with Tlaloc – Chalchihuitlicue, goddess of the jade petticoat and elder sister of the rain gods. Her colouring – she was painted blue and yellow and wore a green stone necklace and turquoise earplugs, and a blue cap with a spray of quetzal feathers – gives her a watery shimmer. Her skirt and shift were painted like water, she was ornamented with waterlilies, and she carried clappers which were always a sign of the water deities.

Chicomecoatl, savage snake woman, in charge of man's nourishment, was also a benign goddess ornamented with water flowers and carrying a sun shield. She can be equated with Coatlicue herself, the great earth mother who engenders and nurtures all things. But there were other goddesses on a lower level who were more truly sinister. Chief of these was the terrible Ciuacoatl who, though she was dressed all in white and 'gave men the hoe and the tump line' (the means of labour), went weeping and wailing through the night, forecasting wars and misery. Her face was painted half red, half black, but her horrible appearance was somewhat alleviated by her feather headdress, her golden earplugs, and the turquoise weaving stick she carried. Was she a darker side of Quetzalcoatl, a savage instead of a redeeming serpent? And was perhaps Tlacolteutl, goddess of vice and eater of filth, a dreadful corollary to the impish Tezcatlipoca? Parallel to the four Tezcatlipocas there were four sisters, all of them aspects of Tlacolteutl: Tiacapan the eldest, Teicu, Tlaco, and Xocutzin the youngest. All these were but four faces of a witch who rode a broomstick in true European style only that she went naked except for a peaked hat. The four sisters hovered at the cross-roads of life, ready one supposes to lure the unwary away from their appointed destination. Turning fearfully from their evil influences, men used to go as penitents to Tezcatlipoca, and the priest would speak to the penitent saying: 'Thou hast come into the presence of the god, protector of all. Thou hast come to confess and to deliver thyself of thine evil and corruption. Thou hast come to unburden thyself of thy secrets. Be sure to commit no fault nor sin. Take off thy clothes; show thy nakedness to the god, the protector, our Lord Tezcatlipoca. Being a mortal, probably thou shalt not see the god; probably he will not speak to thee, a mortal. For he is invisible and impalpable. So thou comest to the god to uncover thy secrets and to explain thy way of life and thine actions... May our Lord, protector of all, take pity on thee, stretch forth his arms to thee, embrace thee, carry thee on his back. Be daring, be not timid nor shameful nor bashful.'

Then the penitent said: 'Our Lord, protector of all, who is aware of my evil smell and my vices, in thy presence I remove my clothing and lay bare my nakedness... Can these things be hid and made dark when they are reflected and clear in thy sight?'

Here is evidence that Tezcatlipoca, although the opponent of Quetzalcoatl who often frustrates the redeemer in his desire for the good and holy life, is in himself not evil. Among the goddesses there are truer personifications of evil, each the converse of some higher god, Quetzalcoatl or Tezcatlipoca, due warnings of what may happen when the free energies on the cosmic scene are deliberately distorted and become sin. From them there is no redemption unless the penitent is prepared to strip himself naked, to show himself as he is, without pretence and without concealment. Only then may he be saved. But the positive and negative poles of natural energy are not in themselves the cause of evil. They are simply opposed poles – 'burning water' and 'blossoming war'. By these two paradoxical concepts the Nahuas sought to express the war and conciliation inherent in all natural phenomena.

Tlacolteutl, like earth and fertility goddesses everywhere, has many of the aspects of a witch. In this leaf from the *Codex Fejervary-Mayer* she can be seen on a broomstick. The serpent was coloured red – the Aztec symbol of sex.

The goddess of flowers and love, Xochiquetzal was loved by Tezcatlipoca, who stole her from the rain god Tlaloc. She is seen uttering 'flowery words', characterised by the decorated speech scroll. *Codex Fejervary- Mayer.*

TLOQUE NAHUAQUE

The dual god-above-all seen in the *Codex Zouche-Nuttall*. Though regarded as the bestower of all life the supreme god was too remote for ordinary man. The male-female deity can be seen on the left, seated by the waters – but it is to the rain god and his consort, seated on the right, that the four priests bring offerings.

That is why the gods on the level of the four compass points, the gods belonging to the world of organic life, such as Quetzalcoatl and Tezcatlipoca, are in a sense more important in the Nahua pantheon than Ometeotl, sometimes called Tloque Nahuaque, the dual god-above-all. Even though he is called 'the god of the near and close', he remains to the ordinary man somewhat remote. He is 'invisible as night, impalpable as wind', and the ordinary man likes to see more clearly defined images of his god than the footprints and hands that appear in some Teotihuatecan frescoes. All the same, Tloque Nahuaque is the original bestower of all life, including his own. He is even said to have invented himself. He is the god who feeds us, and the serious seeker after truth must thus regard him as essentially accessible and merciful. The temple to him was all gold and precious feathers within, black and crusted with stars on the outside. His consort is the goddess of the starry petticoat, of all the heavens. There was never a statue of any kind made in his likeness. As Ometeotl, the supreme dual lord and lady, he is described as the Lord of the Ring, 'self-willing, self-enjoying':

Even as He wills, so shall He desire that it shall be.

In the centre of the palm of His hand He has placed us,

He is moving us according to His pleasure.

We are moving and turning like children's marbles, tossed without direction.

To him we are an object of diversion...

From one point of view, it seems a terrible thing for man to be no more than the plaything of the gods; from another, there could be no more kindly fate than to be a child's marble in the hands of the all-powerful.

There was a tendency to bring the great god-above-all down onto a level of visible creation; for example, he may sometimes be identified with the old god, the fire god, his consort becoming the earth or moon. The tribe of the Otomí Indians regarded the dual pair as the parents of five different nations, themselves among them. Even so, they give their great god, whom they call Otonteuctli a headdress representing an obsidian butterfly, symbol of the most complete permanence within the transitory.

In a lesser-known codex (the Huamantla) there is a drawing of Otonteuctli and Xochiquetzal, goddess of flowers but also of the obsidian butterfly, seated together inside a cave. At the top of the arched entrance there is a split or fault, and the inscription reads 'This is the cave from which we came forth'. The impression is of the male and female principles of permanence in transience – of noumena behind phenomena – enclosed in a curved space that looks like a skull. Out of the split at the top of the skull or cave these two energies, male and female, immortal and at the same time ephemeral in all their palpable manifestations, can come forth. In one hymn the god of fire says:

> I tie a rope to the sacred tree.
> I plait it with eight strands so that I –
> a magician –
> may descend to the magical house.
> Intone your song in the Hall of Flames;
> Intone your song in the Hall of Flames.
> Why does the magician not come forth?
> Why does he not appear?
> May his vassals serve him in the Hall of Flames.
> He comes, he comes, let his vassals serve him.

What is this eight-stranded rope by which the god of fire must descend in order to release the magician? It is impossible to answer this question dogmatically, but the whole impression is of a downward plunging of fire, or some primaeval energy, to release the magician, creator of all possibilities in the universe.

More usually, however, the great god-above-all is not concerned with energies and matter, being too distant, too rarified. In his purest form he is never depicted in images, and only his footprints and his hands are permitted to be drawn. It would seem to be impossible to describe his face. He is not to be looked at by human kind. He belongs to a different order, and it is to the gods on a lower level – especially to Quetzalcoatl – that man must turn if he would ask for mercy.

One extant hymn to Quetzalcoatl's successor Huitzilopochtli describes him as 'only a mortal', and in many respects he was. He is also said to be 'a magician, a terror, a disturber of life' – but this is more true of him in his aspect of Tezcatlipoca. His kindlier qualities are closer to those of Cinteotl, the corn god, with whom he is also identified, especially in a hymn that was sung only every eight years when there was a period of fasting on bread and water. Out of the fasting seems to have arisen joy and fertility and plentitude, for the hymn is one of the happiest:

The Maya water goddess Ixchel, seen on a colossal stele from Copán, Honduras. She differs from her Nahua counterpart Chalchiuhuitlicue in being the consort of the chief god of the pantheon, and she is also the goddess of childbirth and weaving.

A game played by the Aztecs was *patolli*, not unlike our game of ludo. This leaf from the *Codex Magliabecchi* shows four players round a board. Macuilxochitl, god of games and feasting, presides.

TLOQUE NAHUAQUE

My heart blossoms and propagates in the middle of the night...
I, Cinteotl, was born in Paradise. I come from the place of flowers.
I am the only flower, the new, the glorious one.
Cinteotl was born of water; as a mortal, as a young man, he was born
 from the sky-blue home of fish. A new, a glorious god.
He shone like the Sun. His mother lived in the house of dawn,
 many-coloured as the quetzal bird, a new and lovely flower.
On earth, even in the market place like any mortal, I – Quetzalcoatl –
 appeared, the great and the glorious.
Be ye happy under the flower-bush, many-coloured like the quetzal bird.
Listen to the quechol bird singing to the gods.
Listen to the quechol singing by the river.
Listen to its flute by the river in the house of reeds.
Would that my flowers might never die. Our flesh is as flowers;
 flowers in the flower land.
He plays ball, plays ball, the servant so marvellously skilled.
He plays ball, the servant highly prized. Mark him. Even he who
 rules over the nobles follows him to his home.
O youths, O youths! Follow the example of your forbears.
Emulate them in the ball court. Establish yourselves in their houses.
She goes to the market place. They carry Xochiquetzal to the market...
She astounds my heart. She astounds my heart.
She has not finished. The priest knows her. She is to be seen
 where the merchants sell ear-rings of jade.
In the place of wonders she is to be seen.
Sleep, sleep, sleep. I fold my hands in sleep. I – a woman – sleep.

Out of the jumble of names here – Cinteotl, Quetzalcoatl, Huitzilo-pochtli (to whom the hymn is said to be dedicated), Xochiquetzal – we may extract the basic message that Quetzalcoatl is the god of fertility and, on a deeper level, of regeneration; Xochiquetzal as well as Quetzalcoatl. This dual principle is born out of the basic element of water, a flower out of the happy land of flowers. It becomes incarnate in human form, and plays ball, the game that teaches mortals how to manipulate the predestined trend of events.

The sudden appearance of Xochiquetzal at the end of the hymn may appear arbitrary. The final stanzas sound like a separate song accidentally strung onto the earlier one; but it must have been part of the fasting ceremony, the final culmination announcing the birth of the goddess of flowers who then sleeps, returns to quiet, returns to her origins.

The sciences of astronomy and mathematics were developed to an extraordinary degree in Mexico, as the remarkable accuracy of their calendars demonstrate. This circular tower at Chichén Itzá is believed to have been part of a Maya observatory.

THE BALL GAME

In every part of old Mexico and Central America, wherever a temple stood, there existed a ball court. They have been found from Honduras to south-eastern Arizona. In the *Annals of Cuauhtitlán* it is said that Topiltzin, the incarnate King Quetzalcoatl, invented the game played in them, but its real age and origin are unknown.

The urge toward symbolic representation was so strongly developed in the Mexican people that every human act, even the games they played, reflected something deeper.

If the interpretation of the ball game as a symbolic working out of man's struggle to master fate seems arbitrary, we should remember the association of games with religious practice and not think of them as mere pastimes, though it is certain that they also provided pleasure. The exact symbolism of the ball game is unknown, but Cottie Burland has suggested that it represents the play of cosmic forces. Since the ball is

A carved stone medallion from Ratinlixul, Guatemala. The ball player is Maya and the glyphs surrounding him probably commemorate a festival. Pre-classic Maya, *c.* 750 A.D.

at the mercy of the players, who with elbows and buttocks (not with arms, hands, or feet) must try to send it through one of the stone hoops placed high on the court walls, it seems that there was a loophole for change in the cycle of heavenly movements. In one of the very few ancient poems that mentions the ball game, there is a suggestion of this free will within the predestined motion of the heavenly bodies. A sacred pheasant, representing the sun, hesitates at a crossroads wondering which road to take:

> Above the field of the ball game
> beautifully the peerless Pheasant sings:
> he is answering the Corn God.
> Now sing our friends,
> now sings the peerless Pheasant:
> at night the Corn God shone.
> 'Only he who wears bells on his ankles
> shall hear my song.
> Only she shall hear my song
> whose face is masked,
> the sign of the new year beginning.
> I give the law in Tlalocan
> I am the purveyor of riches.
> I am the purveyor in Tlalocan.
> I give the law.
> Oh, I have reached the point
> where the road divides:
> I am the Corn God!
> Where shall I go?
> Where continue my road...?'

The usual interpretation of the ball game is more sanguinary, and is based partly on frieze sculptures apparently showing the captain of the losing team beheaded, with blood spurting from seven vessels. The game, according to this view, was a physical battle. So too are football or tennis. But games have a symbolic origin, the pre-Hispanic ball-game no less than snakes and ladders, which had incidentally its ancient American counterpart in *patolli*, played on a crossshaped 'board' drawn out on the ground.

The symbolic nature of the game is evident in a story of how Quetzalcoatl played one day against Tlaloc the rain god and his children. Quetzalcoatl won, and Tlaloc offered him maize as his prize; but Quetzalcoatl would have nothing less than jade and fine feathers. Tlaloc gave him these, but warned him that jade could not compare in value with maize as food for man. Maize – organic and growing – was more appropriate a reward for victory than petrified jade.

Here a warning is needed. The symbolism of the ancient myths can never be regarded as rigid. Jade and precious stones seem sometimes to represent atrophy and loss of life, at others the fixing of spiritual qualities in the 'deified heart' so that it is no longer transient, like a flower or a butterfly, but endures like some precious or semi-precious stone. Nothing in the Quetzalcoatl symbolism is static. Everything is moving, everything is changeable, and in interpreting its many facets one has always to be watchful of the total context, remembering that the aim is the creation of man in the fullest sense of the word, 'man made man' as one poem has it: man with all his potential fulfilled.

MAYA PARALLELS
WITH THE NAHUA GODS

Quetzalcoatl's religion extended into the Maya lands to the south and became confounded with that of the authors of the *Chilam Balam* and the *Popol Vuh*. But this was possible only because there was already a similarity in their thinking. The Maya god above all, sometimes known as Hunab-ku (the Great Hand, the God Behind the Gods, invisible and impalpable), is the exact parallel of Ometeotl (or Tloque Nahuaque). Quetzalcoatl was translated by the Mayas into Kukulcan, but was also identical with the earlier Itzamná, son of Hunab-ku. Itzamná introduced maize and cocoa into the human diet. He also saw the usefulness of rubber, invented writing, and generally established culture just as his Nahua counterpart had done further north.

The Bacabs, deities of the four compass points, who were placed there to give the world a firm support, seem to be the Maya equivalents of the four Tezcatlipocas, or Quetzalcoatl and three Tezcatlipocas. Each had personal names: Kan (yellow), Chac (red), Zac (white), and Ed (black). They had also the generic name Balam and were linked with the four winds.

Kinich Ahau is the fire bird, or Quetzalcoatl as sun god. Chac is the equivalent of Tlaloc, god of rain. Yum Kaax is the Maya corn god, and so on through the whole pantheon – which makes one suppose (though

A leaf from one of the rare Maya sacred books, *Codex Tro-Cortesianus*, showing the maize god, left, and the rain god Chac, right.

Left: a Mayan ball player, attired with elaborate yoke at his waist and wearing a headdress. He is probably performing a ritual in honour of the sun god before the game begins. The god of death can be seen in the lower right-hand corner. Monument III from the island of Cozumel, *c.* 1000 A.D.

Right: the Maya god of death, God 'A', seen holding a death's head in his hands. Painted pottery figure from Tikal, Guatemala.

A stone sculpture from Quiché, Guatemala, of the mask of Itzamná, the Maya god-above-all sometimes identified with Quetzalcoatl. He gave the Mayas cocoa and maize and invented writing.

the special protagonists of one or other religion will not have it so) that the Maya and the Nahua deities came originally from a single source possibly further back than either. Certainly there was no basic difference in the two systems of thought, both of which point to the need for refining man's emotions until they are capable of praising the creator – as in the Maya myth of creation – or of forming a deified heart as in the Nahua philosophical concept.

The name Mayapan, given to the Maya New Empire which endured from 987 to 1697 A.D., means 'the Standard of the Not Many', from Maya (not many) and pán (standard). It was sometimes called Ichpa, meaning 'within the enclosure', an exactly parallel idea to the Nahua description of Tloque Nahuaque as Lord of the Ring.

Like the Nahuas, the Mayas had an hierarchical caste system related to their gods. There were the ruling intellectual nobility on the one hand, and the priestly caste of the Sun on the other. Each of these hierarchies was in turn split into different grades according to their degree of advancement in religious and civic understanding. At the very top were the priests of Kukulcan (Quetzalcoatl). Immediately underneath these were the caste of nobles known as the *Halach uinic*, meaning 'true man', and the priestly caste *Ahuacan*, lord serpent. The 'true men' sat in judgment on those rising in the caste system in order to decide which among them should qualify to be *Almenhenob*, 'those who had fathers and mothers'. Evidently the parents referred to are the true men themselves, and in order to qualify as sons of these high men it was necessary to possess the key to a special language called *Zuyua* – the language of the Xiu people.

The Xiu were an important ruling Maya family centered in Uxmal and one member of it, Ah Kukum Xiu, helped Francisco Montejo the younger in his conquest of Yucatán. The language to which the Xiu gave their name may well have been much older and more venerable than the family itself.

The 'true men' who were the 'fathers and mothers' of lesser mortals, carried in their right hands a sceptre in the shape of a mannikin, one leg ending in a serpent which is the sceptre's handle. In the left hand they carried a shield of the sun god, seal and proof of their high status.

The *Almenhenob*, children of the 'true men' had their parallel in the priestly hierarchy: *Chilanes*, or diviners. The *Almenhenob* could be either hereditary or elected, but all the *Nacom* were elected for three years during which time they could have no relations with women, not even with their wives; they could not eat red meat, must not get drunk, and were not served by any woman. They lived in a place apart, with their own special cooking utensils. The *Nacom* were the lowest order of priesthood but on the lay side there was a caste called 'those at the head of the mat', *Ah holpopoh*, who stood in an intermediary position between the nobles and the common people. Their name suggests that they presided at ordinary gatherings consisting of the three lowest castes: the *tupiles* (town constables), the common people, and the slaves. All these lived outside the towns and villages, so that the distance of a man's house from the central plaza showed his position in the social-religious scale.

Somewhere at the level of Kukulcan were a host of other gods who are usually known to modern scholars only as a series of initials. God A is Hunhau or Ahpuch, the god of death who ruled over Mitnal, a name similar to the Nahua death country Mictlan. Hunhau is sometimes represented with a human body and the head of an owl, and present-day Indians of Mexico and Central America believe that when the owl screeches somebody will die.

The Mayan god of sacrifice, God 'F'. He is also a warrior god, and his distinguishing mark is the line encircling the eye and extending down over his cheek. Temple carving from Kabah.

Below: a clay statuette from the Veracruz region. This ball player is simply attired but common to all is the heavy waistband. He carries the ball here, but during the game it was never touched by hand. The ball was made of rubber, and it was a description of the game by Oviedo in the sixteenth century that acquainted Europeans with this unique substance.

The Mayas were as preoccupied with death as the Nahuas, and both peoples believed that suicides went to paradise, not to hell. The Mayas thought they went to the goddess Ixtab, goddess of the noose or gallows. It is tempting to wonder whether originally the idea of suicide was related to the killing of a man's lower nature, whether it is an idea parallel to that of the hanged man of the Tarot pack. In this case the happy after-death fate of suicides would be explained.

Hunhau is usually associated with the dog, who is a symbol of death and the bearer of lightning. The Lacandón Indians, a few of whom still survive in the forests of Chiapas though the race is dying out, still place an image of a dog on their graves. Eduard Seler thought that the dog was buried with men because he had in life been their faithful companion, and that this practice gave rise to the animal's association with death. In the day names of the calendar the dog is the Maya *Oc*, the last day of the series, signifying the lowest point reached by the soul on his spiritual journey. If we take the pilgrimage as beginning with the first day of the Nahua series then *Itzcuintli*, the dog, falls on the same day. The Nahuas and the Mayas evidently had their equivalent of Cerberus.

God B is Kukulcan, the equivalent of Quetzalcoatl and the most important deity in the Maya pantheon. Some characteristics link him also with Tlaloc; and conversely there are other Maya gods that can be associated with Quetzalcoatl in certain particular aspects of his nature.

Kukulcan has a proboscis-like nose and serpent fangs at either side of

A fine stucco head from Tabasco. Remarkable for the European features, the nobility of the face and the unusual beard suggest that it may be a portrait of Kukulcan. Pre-classic Maya.

Below: an ancient Maya stone carving, sixth to ninth centuries, of the god of virility, a rare example of ithyphallic presentation. He was probably an early manifestation of Itzamná.

his mouth. His chief symbol is a torch, or fire; but he has also four others that seem to represent the four elements. They are the sprouting maize (earth), the fish (water), the lizard or salamandar (fire), and the vulture (air). In his heraldry there are four colours that also seem to represent the elements: yellow (air), red (fire), white (water), and black (earth). He sits at the centre of a crossshaped tree, at the centre of the four compass points or of the quincunx. Sometimes he is earthy, planting maize, going on a journey with staff and bundle, and armed with axe and spear. At other times he is watery, being enthroned in clouds or riding in a canoe from which he goes fishing. He alternately devours or is devoured by a serpent. His day is *Ik*, the day of breath and of life, and he never on any account appears in conjunction with the frequent death symbols of Maya mythology. Like Quetzalcoatl he is essentially the god of resurrection and rebirth.

Little is known about god C except that his face is ornamented, that he hangs from the sky by a rope, and that his day is *Chuen*. This is the first created day of the Maya series, when the god-above-all brought forth divinity from himself and created heaven and earth. It is thought that this is a star god and one is inclined to think that he may be the planet Venus, in which case he would be another aspect of Kukulcan (Quetzalcoatl), though some have equated him with the Pole star. However, the more we study the Maya gods the more we find the kaleidoscopic central figure proliferating in a multitude of patterns, as if his full meaning were

Victorious Maya warriors – a detail from one of
the mural paintings at Bonampak. The scene depicted
is probably a successful raid on another tribe to
obtain prisoners for sacrifice.
Right: a head carved in trachite from the stairway
of Temple 26 at Copán, Honduras. It represents the
young maize god Yum Caax and embodies all the
Maya ideals of masculine beauty. Classic Maya style.

too vast for the human mind to grasp entire.

God D, for example, can also be equated with Kukulcan-Quetzalcoatl, though he is an old man with sunken cheeks and a mouth devoid of teeth except for one in the lower jaw. He is god of the Moon and of night, and his day is *Ahau* when bad men go to hell. Contradictorily however he never appears with death symbols. Sometimes he wears on his head a conch shell, symbol of birth and one of the distinctive signs for breath or life. Perhaps he represents the perpetual cycles of death and rebirth.

God E is *Ghanan* or Yum Caax, the maize god, god of the harvest fields, equivalent to the Nahua Cinteotl and thus also an aspect of Kukulcan-Quetzalcoatl. He is a handsome god with the long profile and elongated, flattened forehead cultivated by the Maya aristocracy and found in stone portraits from Palenque and in the paintings of Bonampak.

A carved lintel from Yaxchilán, *c.* 700 A.D. An offering, rather like the medicine bundles of North America, is being presented to a priest in elaborate robes and headdress, probably representing Kukulcan.

Skulls of Maya children were artificially flattened by tying boards to them when the bones were still soft. The resulting long oval shape is said to have represented an ear of maize. God E is associated with life, prosperity, and fruitfulness, never with death.

God F has a resemblance to Xipe, the flayed god. He is distinguished by vertical marks on his face. God G, who is Kukulcan in his aspect of sun god, is at times linked rather oddly with death. He has a snake-like tongue obtruding from his mouth.

God H, with a spot or snake scale on his forehead, seems to be Kukulcan-Quetzalcoatl in his serpent aspect. His day is *Chicchan*, associated with the serpent.

The deity lettered I is female, goddess of water, floods, and cloudbursts. She wears a knotted serpent on her head.

Although god K, with his elephant trunk, has been given a separate letter, he may be one more variant of god B, or Kukulcan. At any rate the two are closely related. God K may have been rather a god-man like Quetzalcoatl in human form. Some workers have identified him with Itzamná, a god who said of himself, 'I am the dew of heaven, I am the dew of the clouds.' He was also called Lakin Chan, serpent of the east, and was said to have been the creator of men and of all organic life and to have founded the Maya culture. He invented writing and books, had a knowledge of herbs and healing, and some say he was the son of Hunab-Ku, the invisible god above all.

God L is old and black with a sunken mouth. He is Ekchuah, god of travellers. God M is a black god with red lips, the lower one large, drooping, almost negroid. He appears to be Ek Ahau, or the black lord, and to have had some connection with war though he was also god of merchants like the Nahua god Yiacatecuhtli.

The headdress of god N bears the sign of the 360-day year, and he is evidently the deity who presides over the year's end. O is female with wrinkles round the eyes, and she is usually represented with a loom. Perhaps she is a goddess of fate. God P is known as the frog god, and he seems to be connected with the calendar, for his headdress, like that of god N, contains the sign for the 360-day year.

Besides these numbered gods there are several others, notably Zotz the bat god, patron of the Zotzil Indians who live today in Chiapas, and of some Guatemalan Indians. The Maya twenty-day period was called Zotz. In Copán there is a relief-carving of a struggle between him and Kukulcan, so that in some ways he seems to be parallel to Tezcatlipoca, opponent of Quetzalcoatl.

There were many Maya war gods, though some may have had a purely symbolic connection with war. Among them are Ahulane the archer, who is shown holding an arrow and whose shrine was on the island of Cozumel; Pakoc, the frightener, and Hex Chun Chan, the dangerous one, both of whom were gods of the usurping Itzá dynasty; Kac-u-Pacat, who carried a shield of fire; Ah Chuy Kak, the fire destroyer; Ah Cun Can, the serpent charmer; and Hun Pic Tok who held eight thousand spears.

Like the Nahuas, the Mayas had their god of intoxication. There was also a god of medicine, Cit Bolon Tum; a god of song, Xoc Bitum; and a god of poetry, Ab Kin Xoc or Ppiz Hiu Tec. The female deities were more benign than the Nahua ones, and included Ix Tub Tun, goddess of workers in jade and amethyst; Chebel Yax who invented woven colour designs; and Ix-huyne, the moon goddess.

The name Aztec means 'the heron people', and may have some bearing on the origins of the tribe which was somewhere to the north of the present boundaries of Mexico. But this stone carving suggests that the heron may have been a symbol in other parts of Mexico; it comes from the Veracruz region where these birds haunt the low-lying marshlands.

Above: the interior of a polychrome bowl with tripod legs. The bird shown here is Moan, the vulture who was the harbinger of death. Late classic Maya.
Right: a Maya vase in the shape of a snail with a figure emerging. It probably represents the wind god, an aspect of Kukulcan in the Maya pantheon just as the Nahua wind god is an aspect of Quetzalcoatl.
Far right: the Maya sun god wearing an elaborate headdress. This presentation of Kinich Ahau appears on a cylindrical carving from Palenque, c. 700 A.D.

THE AZTECS' JOURNEY
TO ANÁHUAC

A relief from Palenque. A triumphant lord, or king, is seated on the prostrate forms of the vanquished, while priests offer him a crown and a sceptre.

We have left until the end of the book the story of the Aztec migration to the land of Anáhuac because this half-history, half-legend fittingly sums up the all-pervading idea of a spiritual pilgrimage from darkness to light. Many historians have interpreted the legend of the arrival of the Aztec people on the high plateau as a simple narrative of events. But the tale is too poetic, and the events take place on too many different levels, for such a literal interpretation to have validity. Even the Aztecs, a barbarous people from the north who later took over the culture, the language, and the religion of the high plateau, had an understanding of the place of legend in history, and knew that myth and symbolism can and should be larger than life.

According to Francisco Xavier Clavijero, who was born near the beginning of the eighteenth century in Veracruz, the Aztecs came from somewhere far to the north of the Colorado river. Their migration southward was instigated by a bird who sang to them from a tree, calling *tihui* – which in the Aztec tongue means 'let us go'. Following upon the bird's

130

instructions, the elders called Tecpaltzin, 'a distinguished man', who told them that they ought indeed to go looking for another homeland. About 1160 the Aztecs set out, and after crossing the Colorado river they made an image of their war god, or sun god, Huitzilopochtli, and placed this on a chair of rushes. Servants of the god, priests working in relays of four, carried this image at the head of the migrating caravan, which consisted of seven sub-tribes including the Mexicans. At one stage a test was made of their understanding. The tribes were presented with two bundles, in one of which was a jewel and in another only sticks. Those who chose the bundle with the sticks were the wisest, the moral being that utility is better than beauty. Or so Clavijero tells us; it is rather an odd thesis to be sustained by a people who wove so much myth about their daily lives. The moral may really go deeper.

Six of the travelling tribes went directly to the land of Anáhuac – the 'place within the ring'. The Mexicans, however, like Peer Gynt, seemed determined to go 'round and about'. After spending some years in Tollan they finally reached Zumpango in the Valley of Mexico in 1216. The ruler of this place, a man called Tochpanecatl, asked the Mexicans if they would provide a wife for his son, Ilhuicatl. A marriage was arranged and the royal house of Mexico was established.

Some of this, evidently, is history; but the story is interlocked with strands of pure mythology. The task of the pilgrims is to find a site where an eagle with a snake in its mouth will be sitting on a nopal cactus in the midst of a lake. This suggests a symbolism of time dominated by some higher force (the snake eaten by the eagle) at the centre of the universe.

Huitzilopochtli speaks to his subjects and tells them (in the transcription by Alfonso Caso, the Mexican anthropologist):

'Verily I shall lead you where you must go. I shall appear as a white eagle; and wherever you go, you shall go singing. You shall go only where you see me, and when you come to a place where it shall seem to me good that you stay, there I shall alight, and you shall see me there. Therefore in that place you shall build my temple, my house, my bed of grasses – where I have come to rest, poised and ready for flight. And in that place the people shall make their home and their dwelling. Your first task shall be to beautify the quality of the eagle, the quality of the tiger, the Holy War, the arrow and the shield. You shall eat what you have need of. You shall go in fear. As payment for your courage you shall conquer, you shall destroy all the villages and hamlets that are there already, wherever you see them...'

We note that the pilgrims of the sun god have a very specific and high task: '...to beautify the quality of the eagle, the quality of the tiger, the Holy War, the arrow and the shield'. It has been a gross misunderstanding to equate the 'holy' war with the later bloodthirsty ones by which the Aztecs held the surrounding tribes in subjection. The holy war was not this, but a psychological war waged within the consciences of specially chosen men capable of conquering their own lower natures.

The pilgrims, evidently chosen people in this spiritual sense, were rewarded by being shown a place of dazzling whiteness. They saw a white cypress tree from which issued a fountain, and all around were white willows, white reeds and bullrushes, white frogs, white fish, white watersnakes. This is certainly not a description of any geographical site on the high Mexican plateau, where rich greens and bright colours abound and white is notably absent.

When the priests and elders saw the place, they wept for joy and said: 'Now we have reached the promised land, now we have seen what

A detail of one of the colossal stone warriors at Tula, Hidalgo, Mexico.
The people of Guatemala believed that they came from 'the place of the sun', and the name Tula, which in various forms is given to a number of cities in Mesoamerica, had that meaning.

comfort and rest has been bestowed upon the Mexican people. Nothing more remains for us. O be comforted, sons and brothers, for we have now discovered and achieved what our God promised you, for He told us we should see wonders among the bullrushes and reed grasses of this place, and lo, these are they. But brothers, let us be silent and return to the place whence we came, and wait for our God's command, and He shall tell us what we have to do.'

Then Huitzilopochtli told them: 'O Mexicans, here must be your task and your office, here must you keep guard and wait, and the four quarters of the earth you must conquer, win, and subject to yourselves. Have command of body, breast, head, arms, and strength, for likewise it shall cost you sweat, work, and pure blood, if you are to reach and enjoy the fine emeralds, the stones of much value, the gold and silver, the fine

A wooden drum of the *teponaztli* type, much used in beating ceremonial rhythms. This one is Mixtec, with a year sign on the bottom right-hand corner. Tenth to fifteenth centuries A.D. British Museum.

feathers, the precious many-coloured feathers, the fine cocoa which has come from afar, the cotton of many colours, the many sweet-scented flowers, the different kinds of soft and delectable fruits, and many other things that give much pleasure and contentment.'

It may appear that we are back on an historical level, with the god offering a paradise of material prosperity. But we still cannot ignore the earlier symbolism, nor the fact that it is the god who is speaking. The eagle, representative of Hiutzilopochtli, is the sun. The nopal cactus with its red fruit is the human heart. The heart and the sun's light are at the centre of man, and from this inner sanctuary they hold Time, the serpent, in its rightful and lowly place. Self-subjection is the task. In ancient Mexican poetry, emeralds signify a fixing of beauty and purity in the human being, as when one poet sings:

> Coral is my tongue
> and emerald my beak:
> I esteem myself highly, my fathers: I, Quetzalchictzin.
> I open my wings
> and weep before my fathers.
> How shall we ever reach the heart of heaven.

It may be objected that the Aztecs arrived late on the scene, and that the symbolism of heart and precious jewel was created long before by the Nahua-speaking people they conquered. However, the narrative of the pilgrimage is retrospective, told by the Aztecs after they had already subdued the people of the high plateau and after they had borrowed a symbolism and a religion from the conquered people.

Thus the story of the pilgrimage has to be read on two levels, and on

one of these it is a beautiful example of Nahua practical mysticism – one more version of the recurring theme of death in the outer, phenomenal world and rebirth on another plane. The thread of the story of a real pilgrimage and war and conquest is often so closely interwoven with the thread of myth that it is difficult to disentangle them; but this does not mean that they are one and the same thing. Huitzilopochtli, who directed the expedition, was a god and was revered in ceremonies of communion in which images of his body were eaten. Amaranth was crushed into a powder, sifted of all chaff and foreign bodies, and made into a dough that was placed in earthen vessels until it was ready to be shaped into the god's image. The priest then pierced the heart of the image, and the body was broken up, to be eaten by the faithful who were known as 'keepers of the god'. Their task was onerous, for they

The great calendar stone of the Aztecs, thirteen feet in diameter, which was discovered in Mexico City on the site of Tenochtitlán. The outer border contains two serpents representing time, within which are the sun's rays. At the centre is the sign Four Motion – the present era, and preceding ages are indicated by the four arms, which also bear the 'motion' sign. The twenty day-names surround the central symbol. The stone was carved just after the year 1502.

The burial chamber in the Temple of the Inscriptions at Palenque, *c.* 700 A.D. The city was founded according to legend by Votan, who was probably a local Maya form of Quetzalcoatl. The carved stone, which depicts the young maize god Yum Caax, weighs more than twenty tons.

A polychrome vase, classic Maya style, showing the god 'N' seated in a conch shell. This was the Maya deity who ruled over the five unlucky inter-calendary days at the end of the year.

had to fast a whole year during which one of their number impersonated Huitzilopochtli and wore his garments. The climax of the feasting was a procession with dancing. One of the penitents marched ahead of the 'god', the others bringing up the rear with pine torches held aloft. In a place called The House of Mist the idol was set down on the floor and flutes were played while offerings of water and grasses were made to him. The image was then bathed, and this ceremony brought the year's penance to an end. From year to year the role of the performers rotated. The man who took the part of the god was called Paynal, he who hastens. He was dressed in a cape and head-ornament made of quetzal feathers. Bars and a star design were painted on his face, and he wore a turquoise nose-plug. On his breast was a shield set with turquoise mosaic, and a mirror.

It is true that in Christendom men have undertaken arduous pilgrimages and have waged wars in the name of their religion and their god, but the conquerors and military leaders have not been the god himself, as with the Mexicans in whose chronicles the worlds of god and man are inextricably interrelated.

The mingling of history and legend can be understood better if we remember a simple fact of human existence often forgotten in the modern, scientific world: that deep truth may exist unrelated to chronology and to material things. The story of the Aztec pilgrimage is history whose psychological and emotional overtones lend it another dimension.

A parallel Guatemalan pilgrimage

Another example of this two-level history common to most ancient peoples is to be found among the Guatemalan Indian tribes called the Cakchiquels of the Xahila family, who say they came 'from over the sea, from Tulan'. They may have come, geographically, from the Nahua lands to the north, where Tulan or Tula existed as an ancient capital. However, we need not take their specified place of origin as necessarily a physical one. The words Tula, Tollan, Tonalan, mean 'the place of the Sun'. The Cakchiquels, then, may have come either from the Nahua lands, or from over the sea to the east or west (sunrise or sunset), or from the metaphorical land of the Sun, of wisdom and knowledge. Their annals say: 'Four men came from Tulan. At the sunrise is one Tullan, and one is at Xibalbay (underworld), and one is at the sunset; and we came from the one at the sunset, and one is where God is.'

Although this suggests that they came physically from the west, they must in their own minds have had a connection with the man who came 'from where God is'; for the chronicle goes on to tell the old story of how the deities made various experiments to create a being who could honour and praise them. Finally he evolved the creature called man, ancestor of all people on earth including the Cakchiquels:

'And now the Obsidian Stone is created by the precious Xibalbay, the glorious Xibalbay, and man is made by the Maker, the Creator. The Obsidian Stone was his sustainer, when man was made in misery, when man was given shape. He was nurtured on wood, he was nurtured on leaves. He desired only the earth. He could not speak, he could not walk. He had no blood, he had no flesh.'

The obsidian stone seems here to represent the solid structure of material life upon which man is based. But man's nourishment was not yet satisfactory for he could not continue to live on wood and leaves. Once again, as in the story of Quetzalcoatl, a search had to be made for a more specifically human food.

A coyote was cleaning his maize field when a hawk called Tiuh Tiuh killed him. The hawk obtained the blood of a serpent and a tapir and kneaded the maize with these ingredients. This was how the flesh of man was formed. For the creation of man it was necessary to kill the lower animal, the coyote, and to incorporate into the maize the blood of the serpent, representing our instinctive nature perhaps, and the tapir.

After this food had been obtained, thirteen men and fourteen women were created and they multiplied. The obsidian stone was made to become 'the enclosure of Tulan' guarded by the Zotzils, the bat people who can see in the night. The human beings were separated into thirteen divisions of warriors and seven tribes. 'Sleep not, rest not, my daughters, my sons,' they were told, 'for to you, the seven rulers, I shall give power in equal shares.' And again, 'Great shall be your burden. Sleep not, rest not, be not cast down, my sons. You shall be rich. You shall be powerful. Let your round shields, your bows and your bucklers be your riches.'

However, a bird living in Tulan and called 'the guardian of the ravine' prophesied their extinction. An owl also declared himself an evil portent, but they refused to believe him. A parakeet foretold their death, but they answered, 'No, you are only the sign of spring.'

All the warriors of the seven tribes reached the sea but were unable to cross it. The two eldest sons called Gagavitz and Zactecauh fell asleep and were conquered. However, these two sons, the heroes of the migration, had in their possession a red staff which they had brought with them from Tulan. They drove it into the sea and caused sand and sea to separate so that a line of firm ground appeared above and below the waters, and they were able to pass across to the far shore.

As related in the annals, the subsequent adventures of the pilgrims seem to have been more or less historical until they met the 'spirit' or 'heart' of the forest, the fire spirit called Zakiqoxol, who was a robber and killer of men. The two warriors would have liked to do away with him, but they deferred to his supernatural quality and his title; instead of trying to destroy him they gave him clothing and a blood-red dagger and shoes. With these he descended into the forest:

'Then there was a disturbance among the trees, among the birds. One

Jadeite stilettos representing the head and beak of a humming bird. Acts of self mutilation were practised for many centuries by the peoples of ancient Mexico, blood probably being drawn from the tongue or the ears. The humming bird was associated with Huitzilopochtli in Aztec times. Olmec jadeite carvings.

could hear the trees speak and the birds call. If we listened we could hear them say "What is this we hear? Who is this?" Therefore that place is called the Place of Restlessness.'

Zakiqoxol seems to be one more representation of the powerful instinctive energy deep in the forest of man's being, creating disquiet within him.

After this the brothers met a nobleman who told them, 'You have come to be the stone scaffolding and the prop of my house. I will give you lordship...' But later Zactecauh suffered an accident, leaving Gagavitz to continue alone. Like those of the Mexicans, the journeyings of this tribe seem to have had a round-and-about quality. For the second time they arrived at a particular mountain described, like the scenery met by the Aztecs, as white. It must have been volcanic, for it spewed fire throughout an entire year. Only Gagavitz and a personage named Zakitzunun

The eagle, the sun, draws life from the serpent, the earth. Life itself is represented by the rapid animated rabbit. The sun and war god of the Aztecs was Huitzilopochtli, and the Knights-Eagle were under his patronage. *Codex Vaticanus.*

dared go forward. All this has the quality of straight history, but suddenly we are back in the land of legend, with Gagavitz spending a lone vigil on the mountain. As the day faded, the courage of those waiting died in their hearts. Only a few sparks descended to where they were.

But suddenly their hero appeared from inside the mountain, so that all the warriors cried out, 'Truly his power, his knowledge, his glory and majesty are terrible. He died, yet he has returned.' So Gagavitz was acknowledged to have conquered the heart of the mountain, that mysterious creature who had descended into the forest with his red dagger and shoes: 'When the heart of the mountain is opened the fire separates from the stone...'

From this point on the chronicle is mainly historical, but the tradition of a holy origin in the place of the sun was not lost. Speaking of one of the tribe's rulers, the document says, 'Not only was he a king in majesty, but he impressed by his learning and the depth of his spirit, derived from Tullan.'

The origins were always in this centre, geographical or legendary, from whence all knowledge came, and the history derived from these origins was always more important to pre-Hispanic peoples than the simple statement of events.

The travels of Votan

The wanderings of Quetzalcoatl plainly come into the same category as these half-historical, half-mythical tales of journeys. There is one Maya tale about the travels of one, Votan, who seems to have been none other than Quetzalcoatl himself and who declared himself to be 'a serpent'. From some unknown origin he was ordered by the gods to go to America to found a culture. So he departed from his home, called Valum Chivim and unidentified, and by way of the 'dwelling of the thirteen snakes' he arrived at Valum Votan. From there he travelled up the Usumacinta river and founded Palenque. Afterwards he made several visits to his native home, on one of which he came upon a tower which was originally planned to reach the heavens but which was destroyed because of a 'confusion of tongues' among its architects. Votan was, however, allowed to use a subterranean passage in order to reach 'the rock of heaven'.

This Votan was supposed to be guardian of the hollow wooden instrument called *tepanaguaste* which is similar to the Mexican *teponaztli* drum. He was greatly venerated and was called by some 'the heart of the cities'. His consort was Ixchel, the rainbow, but she was sometimes known as Ix-kanleom, the spider's web catching the morning dew.

Votan's priests were of the caste of 'tigers' as Quetzalcoatl's were; and it is evident that he was a great enough leader to have extended his religious beliefs through a vast Maya-Nahua territory, so that they endured for many centuries, only gradually becoming distorted from their original redeeming message. It is a universal tragedy that we know so little of this great religious leader, Quetzalcoatl-Kukulcan-Votan: plumed serpent, quetzal bird, Venus and sun god, who sacrificed himself that true manhood might be created in the hemisphere of the west.

In spite of the great gulf that separates precolumbian thought from our own in many of its external aspects; in spite of distortions, irrelevancies, decadence and subsequent annihilation by European conquerors of a great part of it; the culture which this mysterious leader established shines down to our own day. Its message is still meaningful for those who will take the trouble to make their way, through the difficulties of outlandish names and rambling manuscripts, to the essence of the myth.

Detail from one of the frescoes at Bonampak. A priest is being arrayed as the plumed serpent, Kukulcan or Quetzalcoatl.

One of the elaborately carved lintels from Menché.
The standing figure is probably a priest (the
headdress suggests the plumed serpent – Kukulcan
to the Mayas) and the kneeling one a penitent.
The date of the inscription corresponds to 223 A.D.
of our era.

FURTHER READING LIST

Asturias, Miguel Angel. *Hombres de Maiz*. Losada, Buenos Aires, 1957.

Burland, Cottie A. *Art and Life in Ancient Mexico*. Bruno Cassirer Ltd., Oxford, 1947.

The Gods of Mexico. Eyre & Spottiswoode, London, 1967.

Magic Books of Mexico. Penguin Books, Harmondsworth, 1953.

Bushnell, G. H. S. *Ancient Arts of the Americas*. Thames & Hudson, London, 1965.

Caso, Alfonso. *The Aztecs, People of the Sun*. Oklahoma Univ. Press, 1958.

Castellanos, Rosario. *The Nine Guardians*. Faber & Faber, London, 1959.

Coe, Michael D. *Mexico*. Thames & Hudson, London, 1962.

The Maya. Thames & Hudson, London, 1966.

Collis, Maurice. *Cortés and Montezuma*. Faber & Faber, London, 1954.

Diaz, Bernal. *The Conquest of New Spain* trans. by J. M. Cohen. Penguin Classics, Harmondsworth, 1963.

Goetz, D. and Morley, S. G. *Popol Vuh* trans. from the Spanish of Adrián Recinos. William Hodge, London, 1951.

Grimal, P. (Ed.). *Larousse World Mythology*. Paul Hamlyn Ltd., London, 1965.

Hagen, Victor W. von. *The Ancient Sun Kingdoms*. Thames & Hudson, London, 1962.

Lothrop, S. K., Foshag, W. F., and Mahler, Joy. *Pre-Columbian Art*. Phaidon Press, London, 1958.

MacCulloch, John A. and Gray, Louis H. *The Mythology of all Races*. 13 vols. Cooper Square Pubs. Inc., New York, 1922.

Morley, S. G. *The Ancient Maya*. Oxford Univ. Press, 1946.

Nicholson, Irene. *Firefly in the Night*. Faber & Faber, London, 1959.

The X in Mexico. Faber & Faber, London, 1965.

Parkes, H. Bamford. *The History of Mexico*. Eyre & Spottiswoode, London, 1962.

Peterson, Frederick. *Ancient Mexico*. Allen & Unwin, London, 1959.

Séjourné, Laurette. *Burning Water*. Thames & Hudson, London, 1957.

El Universo de Quetzalcoatl. Fondo de Cultura Económica, Mexico, 1962. (*The Universe of Quetzalcoatl*.)

Soustelle, Jacques. *Daily Life of the Aztecs* trans. by Patrick O'Brian. Weidenfeld & Nicolson, London, 1961.

Thompson, J. E. *The Rise and Fall of Maya Civilisation*. Oklahoma Univ. Press, 1956.

Vaillant, G. C. *The Aztecs of Mexico*. Penguin Books, Harmondsworth, 1952.

Wuthenau, A. von. *Altamerikanische Tonplastik*. Holle Verlag, Baden–Baden. (An English edition is in preparation. Methuen & Co. Ltd., London.)

ACKNOWLEDGMENTS

For permission to quote an extract from *The Nine Guardians* by Rosario Castellanos (translated from the Spanish by Irene Nicholson), the Nahua poems on pp. 75, 114-5, 118 and 132, from *Firefly in the Night*, by Irene Nicholson, and the latter's translations of passages from *Coatlicue, estética del arte indígena antiguo* by Justino Fernández (Centro de Estudios Filosóficos, Mexico, 1954) and *El Pueblo del Sol* by Alfonso Caso (Fondo de Cultura Económica, Mexico) on pp. 85 and 131, the publishers gratefully acknowledge Messrs Faber & Faber Ltd.

The publishers also acknowledge the following sources for permission to reproduce the illustrations indicated.

Colour plates: British Museum: 36. Dumbarton Oaks, Robert Woods Bliss Collection: 86, 101, 125, 128 *top*. Arpad Elfer: *front cover*. Fondo Editorial de la Plástica Mexicana: 77. Giraudon: 55. Irmgard Groth-Kimball: *frontispiece*, 59, 76, 80, 81, 97, 100, 128 *bottom*. Eugen Kusch: 121. Constantino Reyes-Valerio: *back cover*, 29, 33, 108, 129. Peabody Museum, Harvard University: 124. Paul Popper: 50, 84. Henri Stierlin: 25, 51. Württemburgisches Landesmuseum, Stuttgart: 104.

Black and white: Paul Almasy: 126 *bottom*. American Museum of Natural History: 27, 53 *top*, 93. Biblioteca Apostolica Vaticana: 45. Bodleian Library, Oxford: 67. British Museum: 68 *bottom*, 136 *top*, 137. The Brooklyn Museum: 82, 83. City of Liverpool Museums: 69, 92, 94, 102-3, 105, 110 *centre, bottom*. Cleveland Museum of Art: 62. Dumbarton Oaks, Robert Woods Bliss Collection: 12 *bottom*, 17, 34 *bottom*, 47, 52, 99, 134 *bottom*, 135. Fondo Editorial de la Plástica Mexicana, Mexico City: 30 *bottom*, 43, 58, 64, 65, 71, 72, 90. Giraudon: 14, 21, 31 *top*, 75 *top*, 88, 95, 107, 122 *bottom*, 123 *bottom*. Raúl Flores Guerrero: 110 *top*. Paul Hamlyn Library: 15, 16, 24, 48-9, 54, 68 *top*, 86, 116, 132. Irmgard Groth-Kimball: 13, 18 *top*, 26 *top*, 28, 30 *top*, 31 *bottom*, 35, 44, 56, 57, 60, 63, 66, 70, 74, 79, 96, 98, 110, 114, 115, 126 *top*. Eugen Kusch: 23 *bottom*, 53 *bottom*, 109, 111, 117, 119, 131. Librairie Larousse: 32, 91. Museo de Antropologia de la Universidad Veracruzana, Jalapa: 26 bottom, 42. Museum of the American Indian, Heye Foundation: 38, 120. Museum für Völkerkunde, Berlin: 118. Museum für Völkerkunde, Vienna: 78. Faber & Faber: *endpapers*, 12 *top*, 61. Peabody Museum, Harvard University: 84. Philadelphia Museum, Arensberg Collection: 89. Paul Popper: 122 *top*. Constantino Reyes-Valerio: 133, 18 *bottom*, 23 *top*, 73, 85, 87, 123 *top*, 136 *bottom* Rijksmuseum voor Volkenkunde, Leiden: 22. Roger-Viollet: 10. Kurt Stavenhagen: 127. Henri Stierlin: 11, 19, 20, 34 *top*, 37, 39, 40 *top*, 102 *bottom*, 106, 111, 112, 130, 134 *top*.

INDEX

Figures in italics refer to illustrations